How Capitalism Forms Our Lives

By using the concept of capitalism as a "form of life", the authors in this volume reconceive capitalism, its mechanisms and effects on our bodies and on our common life.

The idea that capitalism is more than a discrete economic system and instead a "form of life" that shapes our relationships with others, our sense of ourselves and our capacities, practices, bodies, and actions in the material world should be rather obvious. Yet efforts – whether through criticism or policy remedies – to redress the vast inequalities, inherent exploitation, alienation, and the manifold destructive effects of capitalism on the environment, typically proceed without grappling fully with the entwinement of the economic with the social and cultural, much less the ethical, ontological, and phenomenological. This volume proposes "form of life" as a heuristic tool, connecting literatures that often remain isolated from one another – the Frankfurt School, neo-materialism, Wittgenstein's philosophy, Foucault's and Agamben's biopolitics, and Marx's discussion of reproduction. In emphasizing economic *practices*, as opposed to capitalism as a system, they conceive of "the economic" as an integral and integrated dimension of life, and thus develop new possibilities for critique. Viewing human beings as "economic bios," provides a needed alternative to analyses that position neoliberalism as an economic logic imposed upon the social and cultural.

This book was originally published as a special issue of the *Journal for Cultural Research*.

Alyson Cole is Professor of Political Science, Gender Studies, and American Studies at Queens College and the Graduate Center at the City University of New York (CUNY), USA. She is the author of *The Cult of True Victimhood: From the War on Welfare to the War on Terror* (2007), and co-editor of *Michael Paul Rogin: Derangement and Liberalism* (2019).

Estelle Ferrarese is Professor of Moral and Political Philosophy at Picardie-Jules-Verne University, France. Her authored and edited books include *Vulnerability and Critical Theory* (2018), *La fragilité du souci des autres: Adorno et le care* (2018), *The Politics of Vulnerability* (2017), and *Éthique et politique de l'espace public: Jürgen Habermas et la discussion* (2015).

I0894914

How Capitalism Forms Our Lives

Edited by
Alyson Cole and Estelle Ferrarese

Routledge
Taylor & Francis Group
LONDON AND NEW YORK

First published 2020
by Routledge
2 Park Square, Milton Park, Abingdon, Oxon, OX14 4RN

and by Routledge
605 Third Avenue, New York, NY 10017

First issued in paperback 2021

Routledge is an imprint of the Taylor & Francis Group, an informa business

British Library Cataloguing in Publication Data
A catalogue record for this book is available from the British Library

Typeset in Myraid pro
by Newgen Publishing UK

Publisher's Note
The publisher accepts responsibility for any inconsistencies that may have arisen during the conversion of this book from journal articles to book chapters, namely the inclusion of journal terminology.

ISBN 13: 978-0-367-78568-0 (pbk)
ISBN 13: 978-0-367-32224-3 (hbk)

Contents

Citation Information

The chapters in this book were originally published in the *Journal for Cultural Research*, volume 22, issue 2 (June 2018). When citing this material, please use the original page numbering for each article, as follows:

Chapter 1

How capitalism forms our lives
Alyson Cole and Estelle Ferrarese
Journal for Cultural Research, volume 22, issue 2 (June 2018) pp. 105–112

Chapter 2

The state of contemporary social philosophy and the tasks of an institute for social research (1931)
Max Horkheimer
Journal for Cultural Research, volume 22, issue 2 (June 2018) pp. 113–121

Chapter 3

Economy as social practice
Rahel Jaeggi
Journal for Cultural Research, volume 22, issue 2 (June 2018) pp. 122–125

Chapter 4

The use of bodies. Agamben's idea of a non-capitalist form of life
Estelle Ferrarese
Journal for Cultural Research, volume 22, issue 2 (June 2018) pp. 126–136

Chapter 5

Universal alienation
David Harvey
Journal for Cultural Research, volume 22, issue 2 (June 2018) pp. 137–150

Chapter 6

The enduring regulation of the poor
Frances Fox Piven
Journal for Cultural Research, volume 22, issue 2 (June 2018) pp. 151–153

Chapter 7

Governmentality, subjectivity, and the neoliberal form of life
Daniele Lorenzini
Journal for Cultural Research, volume 22, issue 2 (June 2018) pp. 154–166

Chapter 8

The subject of objects: Marx, new materialism, & queer forms of life
Alyson Cole
Journal for Cultural Research, volume 22, issue 2 (June 2018) pp. 167–179

Chapter 9

The whiteness of capital
Victoria Hattam
Journal for Cultural Research, volume 22, issue 2 (June 2018) pp. 180–185

Chapter 10

Beyond the barricades: class interests and actually existing black life
Cedric G. Johnson
Journal for Cultural Research, volume 22, issue 2 (June 2018) pp. 186–190

Chapter 11

The capitalist metabolism: an unachieved subsumption of life under the value-form
Timothée Haug
Journal for Cultural Research, volume 22, issue 2 (June 2018) pp. 191–203

Chapter 12

Vocabularies of vulnerability
Sharon P. Holland
Journal for Cultural Research, volume 22, issue 2 (June 2018) pp. 204–208

Notes on Contributors

Alyson Cole is Professor of Political Science, Gender Studies, and American Studies at Queens College and the Graduate Center at the City University of New York (CUNY), USA. She is the author of *The Cult of True Victimhood: From the War on Welfare to the War on Terror* (2007), and co-editor of *Michael Paul Rogin: Derangement and Liberalism* (2019).

Estelle Ferrarese is Professor of Moral and Political Philosophy at Picardie-Jules-Verne University, France. Her authored and edited books include *Vulnerability and Critical Theory* (2018), *La fragilité du souci des autres: Adorno et le care* (2018), *The Politics of Vulnerability* (2017), and *Éthique et politique de l'espace public: Jürgen Habermas et la discussion* (2015).

David Harvey is Distinguished Professor of Anthropology & Geography and the Director of Research for the Center for Place, Culture and Politics at the Graduate Center of the City University of New York (CUNY), USA. He has been teaching Karl Marx's *Capital* for over 40 years.

Victoria Hattam is Professor of Politics at The New School, USA. She has long-standing interests in political economy and identity. Her research focuses on American political thought and culture, American political economy, and American political development.

Timothée Haug is a PhD candidate in Philosophy at the Université de Strasbourg, France. His current work focuses on the ecological transformation of Marxist theory. He served as a Visiting Scholar at the Centre Marc Bloch in Berlin, Germany, where he co-organized with Estelle Ferrarese the international workshop 'The Form that Capitalism Gives to our Lives'.

Sharon P. Holland is the Townsend Ludington Term Distinguished Endowed Professor in American Studies at the University of North Carolina at Chapel Hill, USA. She blogs on food, writing, and all things equestrian. She is the editor of *South: A Scholarly Journal* (formerly *Southern Literary Journal*).

Max Horkheimer was a German Philosopher and Sociologist. He belonged to the Frankfurt School of Social Research. The main focus of his work was Critical Theory, a movement which he founded and developed.

Rahel Jaeggi is Professor of Practical Philosophy and Social Philosophy at the Humboldt University of Berlin, Germany. Her areas of specialization include social philosophy and critical theory.

Cedric G. Johnson is Associate Professor of African American Studies and Political Science at the University of Illinois at Chicago, USA. His interests include racial and ethnic politics; African American political thought; neoliberalization; political economy; urban politics; and critical urban theory.

Daniele Lorenzini is a Marie Skłodowska-Curie Cofund 'Move-in-Louvain' Postdoctoral Fellow in the Centre Prospéro at the University of Saint-Louis – Brussels, Belgium, and a Postdoctoral Fellow in the Center for Contemporary Critical Thought at Columbia University, USA. He is a co-editor of the journals *Foucault Studies* and *Materiali Foucaultiani*.

Frances Fox Piven is Distinguished Professor Emeriti in Sociology and Political Science at the Graduate Center of the City University of New York, USA. She is an internationally renowned social scientist, scholar, and activist.

1 How capitalism forms our lives

Alyson Cole and Estelle Ferrarese

Even before 'economic precarity' became the default explanation for the rise of defensive nationalism globally, scholars had already begun returning to ground their work in the economy and materiality more generally. This shift is evident across disciplines, from the expanding field of 'critical economics,' to the popularity of 'capitalism studies,' the emergence of 'neomaterialism,' and the revived interest in Frankfurt school thinkers and even Karl Marx himself, to the push back against the so-called 'linguistic turn' and Foucauldian analyses of power. Despite this renewed attention, the question remains: 'the economy' in what sense?

The idea that capitalism is more than an economic system, and instead, as Marx first framed it, a 'definite mode of life' that shapes our relationships with others, our sense of ourselves and our capacities, practices, and actions in the material world, should be rather obvious. Yet efforts – whether through criticism or policy remedies – to redress the vast inequalities, inherent exploitation, reification and alienation, to say nothing of the manifold destructive effects of capitalism on the environment, typically proceed without grappling fully with the entwinement of the economic with the social and cultural, much less the political, ethical, ontological, and phenomenological. It seems, therefore, that we require new heuristics to comprehend capitalism broadly and deeply, to investigate and further define the work of capital on these multiple registers simultaneously.

In this special issue of the *Journal of Culture Research*, we propose 'form of life' as a possible heuristic. Rather than replace one emphasis (e.g. the discursive) with another (e.g. the material), the concept of a 'form of life' presumes all facets of life are inherently interwoven, bypassing distinctions between discourse, bodies, language, and materiality. It thus enables scholars to incorporate the diverse aspects of life in their analysis, to investigate the effects of capitalism holistically and at a range of scales. While the contributions in this volume vary in their focus and align with different theoretical approaches and methodologies, all provide meditations on the scope, contours, and content of capitalism as a form of life.

The concept 'form of life' comes from the German '*Lebensform*.' In the German language, there is another semantically similar word that conjures a rather different meaning, '*Lebensweise*,' often translated as a 'way of life' or a 'lifestyle.' Unlike a lifestyle (*Lebensweise*), about which we presume we make purposeful choices, a 'form of life' (*Lebensform*), as Ludwig Wittgenstein clarifies, is part of 'natural history … which no one has doubted, but which have escaped remark only because they are always before our eyes' (1968, p. 415). Hanna

Pitkin, who considers the concept both richly suggestive and frustratingly enigmatic, concisely explicates Wittgenstein's account:

> Human life as we live it and observe it is not just a random, continuous flow, but displays recurrent patterns, regularities, characteristic ways of doing and being, of feeling and acting, of speaking and interacting. Because they are patterns, regularities, configurations, Wittgenstein calls them *forms;* and because they are patterns in the fabric of human existence and activity on earth, he calls them forms *of life*. (1973, p. 132)

While Wittgenstein's formulation of 'meaning is use' is credited as among the earliest theorizations of the concept, references to 'forms of life' abound in the Frankfurt School's critical theory and some branches of anthropology (such as the work of Veena Das and Didier Fassin), as well as in the writings of Stanley Cavell, and even the late Michel Foucault and Giorgio Agamben adopted the concept. Given these diverse applications, seeking a unified meaning would be tricky, and to do so might flatten the concept and the important work it performs in these different contexts. Certainly the social ontology on which the idea of a form of life is built, whether or not this is explicitly defined, diverges from one school of thought to the next. Nevertheless, we propose that the polyphonic topicality this concept currently enjoys is significant: some shared traits exist across these traditions that, through the 'form of life' framing, enable us to grasp phenomena that might otherwise remain illegible.

What is a 'form of life'?

Despite varied uses and inflections, at least four characteristics of a 'form of life' can be traced in most theories drawing upon the concept.

(1) A form of life is not constituted by its content; that is, by some specific combination of features. Instead, it is compromised of the configuration established by the arrangement of features *among* themselves.

A form of life always involves a series of *practices,* and the *work* of sustaining those practices. The concept refers to an assemblage that is 'continually engendered by its own *manner,*' to take one of Agamben's recurrent formulations. The category of 'use' is frequently employed in this context. In Agamben's writings in particular, 'use' designates a human activity that cannot be reduced to either production (it is not manifested in particular modes of labor and there is no end product per se), or praxis (because acting well is not in itself the end). The point is to engage the world, one's body, and so forth, in a manner in which there is no a priori project, principle, or intention being purposefully actualized. As practices, forms of life are configurations of human *co*existence, and thus continually reproduced and modified; rendering them malleable, even destructible.

(2) The notion of a 'form of life' always refers to a *sedimentation* – of ideas, meanings, or ethical content. 'Form of life' describes the gradual aggregation of meaning-laden practices that are, in the course of this process, increasingly made unavailable; that is, rendered inaccessible to simple challenge. A form of life is, therefore, that which establishes or imposes itself, and thereby commands.

This deposit or residue is primarily ethical in nature. Forms of life impregnate the relationships we have to one another, our material world, and therefore ourselves; they constitute the basis of any conceivable idea of the good life.

Theorists who use the concept of a 'form of life' characterise such sedimentation as the residue of past commitments, which then become ossified in institutions and in things. But the expectations that have shaped them continue to linger – a claim lies within them. At the same time, a form of life never appears as a pure obligation or constraint, or even as a simple convention. In Wittgenstein's terms, a 'form of life' is foremost a type of agreement, an 'agreement in judgments' that are necessary for collective life. As Cavell cautions, however, we should not understand this agreement as 'some kind of contract or an implicitly or explicitly agreed upon set of rules' (1989, p. 41). A form of life does not result from a regulated, consensual protocol, whether individual or collective. The agreement is tacit, coinciding with the form itself.

A form of life is, then, always a proposition, a proposal of meaning. This is where politics enters, in particular a politics that refuses this proposition of solidified meaning, that seeks to challenge what is presented as given. Critical theorists, for example, maintain that forms of life have a claim to rationality or validity embedded within them. This claim makes criticising a form of life possible; it is what enables us to evaluate its rationality and validity. As propositions of meaning that deposit themselves and remain in institutions, subjectivities, and daily objects, forms of life respond to the question of 'how we ought to live.' Because they typically respond poorly, they *enable and oblige critique*. Employing the concept of a 'form of life' allows us to investigate and evaluate how we live. It thereby opens the possibility to reflect on how we would like to live and, as importantly, provides the perspective to consider how our form of life delimits or forecloses certain prospects by excluding other forms of life. Put simply, 'form of life' as a heuristic enables us to examine the taken for granted, to break with the comfort of the familiar.

(3) Forms of life have ethical textures. To speak of a 'form of life' thus presumes a concreteness or materiality to political and moral life.

The concept 'form of life' includes affective dispositions and orientations, as well as gestures, facial expressions, and bodily modes of intersubjectivity. The syntagm extends to the idea that there is a properly embodied form of life, which Theodor Adorno sums up in the notion of the 'physiognomy' of the capitalist form of life. A form of life also sediments in legal systems, in modes of kinship, architecture, fashion, and everyday objects. The world in which we engage and perform our moral acts is also a material and institutional arrangement, one that conditions our actions and our life possibilities. This is the core reasoning underpinning *Minima Moralia*. Like Walter Benjamin, Adorno also reminds us that forms of thought are entangled with the most banal objects; such objects bear myths, or incarnate them. And, conversely, they shape and mediate our moral gestures. Using the example of the development of doors in bourgeois interiors, Adorno highlights how self-closing doors permit the person arriving to enter the room uninvited, so that tact and thoughtfulness cannot be rightly understood without also accounting for the door that should be closed quietly (2006, p. 40). As Rahel Jaeggi (2005) subsequently argued, reasoning in terms of 'forms of life' casts the questions of 'how we ought to act' as integrally tied to the prior question of 'what makes us act;' that is, to reflecting on how each social formation has a material reality.

(4) The notion of 'form of life' always seeks to grasp the articulation of the 'social' and the 'vital' on which the institutions of the human world rest.

Identifying human beings as *living beings,* i.e., mortal, sexual beings, lies at the core of the idea of a 'form of life.' It therefore entails reflecting on physiological constitutions, vital processes, and the reproduction of life, including non-human living beings. All theories of forms of life presume that life is lived through the infinite prism of historically produced forms of life, but the concept is not attached to any particular moral or political reasoning or functionalist materialism. It reflects instead a social relation between the living and culture, their embodiment and environment. It thus reveals how the vulnerability of our lives is intrinsically both social and biological, and how human vulnerability cannot be apprehended separately from the vulnerability of non-human lives.

From this perspective, bodies appear as always shaped by practices and, simultaneously, as constituting the materiality that holds and constrains forms of life. Veena Das, for example, has shown in her ethnographic fieldwork on violence in post-partition India how women's bodies repaired a collective form of life, brutally damaged by rape and murder, by swallowing and containing the 'poisonous knowledge' of violence (2007, pp. 59–78). By understanding the political subject as a living being, theories of forms of life consequently require rethinking concepts such as the ordinary and the common, singularity, powerlessness and agency, and politics itself. Such theoretical commitments are especially important for political reflection. The idea of 'forms of life' precludes the possibility of any functional separation between human reproduction and production, thus undermining clear-cut distinctions between the private, social, economic, and political; since all these activities must be seen in terms of their effect on the possibility of human life, the distinctive form that they contribute to making.

Capitalism as a 'form of life'

The essays in this volume attempt to rethink capitalism, its mechanisms, and its effects on our bodies and on our common life. Each essay elaborates central correlates of the concept 'form of life,' whether or not the author explicitly uses the expression. The premise the authors implicitly share is that by redefining capitalism as a form of life, it can be analyzed as a social practice, rather than as a system radically distinct from the cultural, social, political or even biological. When economics is conceived as a discrete activity or sphere, the reciprocal impact of the economy on our lives and our lives on the economy recedes to the background: it appears as isolated and autonomous, a function of instrumental rationality or the market. By emphasising economic *practices*, the notion of a 'form of life' opens productive new ways of conceiving of 'the economic' as an integral and integrated dimension of life, and thus renews possibilities for critique. In turn, regarding human beings as 'economic bios' reveals the plasticity of our economic form of life and its biological and cultural aspects, providing a needed alternative to analyses that position neoliberalism as an economic logic imposed upon the social and cultural, occluding how other areas of life are always intertwined with the economic, though not completely subsumed by it.

We open this volume with Max Horkheimer's inaugural address delivered when he assumed the position of Director of the Frankfurt Institute in 1931, 'The Present Situation of Social Philosophy and the Tasks of an Institute for Social Research.' While this lecture has been published in English before, we were surprised to discover how Horkeheimer's uses and inflections of the words '*Leben*' and '*Lebensform*' are erased in the available translations. In the version included here, we have restored the meaning of '*Lebensform*' thus amplifying Horkheimer's effort to incite social philosophy in general, and critical theory in particular, to examine humans as producers of their historical forms of life. Not all of the authors in this volume draw from critical theory, but each contribution in its own way assumes the ground Horkheimer set forth when he insisted upon the study of comprehensive forms of life in contrast to the 'transfiguring' of metaphysics, on the one hand, and the positivism, scientism, formulaic rationalism and 'chaotic specialization,' on the other.

In her short intervention, 'Economy as Social Practices,' Rahel Jaeggi emphasises that capitalism can only be rightly understood when the economy is analyzed as 'bundle of practices.' She argues that the market and the economy in general must be viewed as subtended by practices endowed with their own normativity. The capitalist form of life, accordingly, results from ethical sedimentation even as it presents itself as ethically neutral.

For Agamben, a form of life cannot, by definition, be capitalist, since capitalism smothers the possibility of all life. In 'The Use of Bodies,' Estelle Ferrarese probes Agamben's effort to imagine a form of life realised through a particular form of 'use,' as a non-instrumental mode of acting, and a withdrawal from the system of power which law organises, namely sovereignty. He presents 'use' and 'law' as incompatible because their respective relationships to bodies cannot be reconciled. Despite a promising focus on embodiment, however, Ferrarese argues that Agamben fails to formulate a critique of the capitalist form of life that adequately addresses the perspective of the living body.

The capitalist form of life responds, as do all forms of life, to the question of knowing how we ought to live, and, according to the Marxian tradition, especially from György Lukacs forward, its response becomes sedimented as a kind of second nature. In Lukacs's formulation this petrification (he depicts it as a 'charnel-house of long-*dead interiorities*') makes it possible to account for the phenomenon of alienation – 'a complex of meanings, which has become rigid and strange' (1971, p. 64). This proposition of meaning, the capitalist form of life, may also be refuted and contested. Placing accumulation by dispossession at the core of his analysis of capitalism, David Harvey's scholarship has always been distinguished by the attention he devotes to capitalism's impact on life, both human and non-human. He consistently shows how a permanent mechanism for pillaging resources and destroying cultures doubles the logic of capitalist exploitation of labor. In his essay for this volume, 'Universal Alienation,' Harvey examines the second nature engendered by this dynamic. The concept of 'alienation' he employs to describe a process exceeding the dispossession of the self and the world, disempowerment, and the affective state of living an alien life, to reveal apathy. Attentive to new commodity chains, the role of value creation, and the replacement of productive capital by financial capital as the driving force of contemporary global and national capitalism, the essay introduces the idea of the trap of 'debt peonage,' which renders all plans for reforming or overthrowing capitalism unaffordable, even unthinkable. This is especially true, he notes, for the intellectual/academic class that is responsible for such plans, but that dare not imperil its major current or prospective source of income – pensions.

What may be inconceivable for precariously privileged intellectuals is the imperative of existence for others. Having spent her illustrious career documenting and combating the disciplining of the poor, Frances Fox Piven's 'The Enduring Regulation of the Poor' exposes how inequality is sedimented in government institutions and policy innovations within the capitalist form of life. She provides a succinct review of how purported efforts to help the poor in fact serve to keep them in poverty and insulate the political process from their existential challenges through which they might alter their lives. Disruptive politics from below has been critical to spurring change at various historical junctures. But Fox Piven traces the steady decline of the policies and infrastructures that have historically supported these movements – dismantled systematically to preserve and sustain capitalism, regardless of the lives left in waste.

In 'Governmentality, Subjectivity, and the Capitalist Form of Life,' Daniele Lorenzini adopts a Foucauldian perspective on how the capitalist form of life imposes itself on the subject. If neoliberalism gives shape to our lives by producing particular subjectivities, these are governed less through the manufacturing of a second nature than by the freedom afforded to subjects. But Foucault also conceives of the form of life as an individual 'uninterrupted practice' that enables access to oneself, and posits the ethical necessity of the subject experiencing her truth at the cost of scandal. In addressing both meanings, Lorenzini's essay outlines the possible ethical conflict between a collective (neoliberal) form of life and a singular form of life realised by the care of the self.

By conceiving of capitalism as a form of life we also view it as a material reality, that is, we grasp it *from* its materiality. Doing so makes it possible to account for how the capitalist form of life produces subjectivities, the social links, forms of thought, and the bodies it requires without recourse to, at least not principally, psychological and ideological motifs. According to Adorno, our form of life, the capitalist form of life, invites a radical diagnosis about the moral life that it shapes, as well as about the critique that it suggests: it makes every life a 'specimen' that only encounters and is only capable of a 'bourgeois coldness,' neutralising critique by presenting itself as given and necessary. This occurs, first, through the generalisation of the exchange-form, which has become the universal form determining all manifestations of life, subjective as well as objective. When he endeavors to shed light on the social causes of bourgeois coldness, Adorno's reflection bears on a generalised and constraining form, rather than on a mystifying discourse or a set of false representations that would compel human beings to adopt attitudes that serve the reproduction of the capitalist order. Indeed, he writes that 'what [individuals] are for themselves, what they think they are is secondary.' (1998, p. 248). The idea of internalising norms or models is grossly mistaken because there is no 'stable subjectivity' of the individual in the capitalist form of life (270). The form transmitted by technologies, commodities, market devices, and mass-medias, replaces it by imposing a reciprocal instrumentalization.

In 'The Subject of Objects,' Alyson Cole reflects on the materiality of our form of life, its ideological consequences, and the current rise of neomaterialism. Elaborating on Marx's conception of the commodity form, she shows that endowing inanimate objects with agency – which neomaterialists presume is their contribution – is precisely a feature of the capitalist form of life. In this regard, she raises crucial questions about the politics of new materialism. As Cole writes, 'the trouble with commodification is less the perversion of the bios than the birth of an alternative and distinctly nonhuman form of life.'

In a similar vein, Victoria Hattam's 'The Whiteness of Capital' traces the hidden transnational mobility of capital, not only through commodity chains but also spatially at the geographic divide between the United States and Mexico. Hattam reveals that this movement is neither obvious nor natural, but continuously performed by political *dispositifs* obscured by politicians' focus on walls and borders. The current preoccupation with the trafficking of bodies and the correlating attempt to curb that flow, she counsels, distracts from the more important movement of capital itself.

Cedric Johnson's intervention considers how the capitalist form of life polices bodies in another context, the rise and expansion of the carceral state and the entwinement of capitalist property with criminality. 'Beyond the Barricades' reflects on how race and racism serve as proxies for both perceiving and redressing inequality in America. Johnson charts the ossification of this racialized framing, a different kind of sedimentation, as a displacement of the economic, thus asking readers to examine the racialized inflections in the capitalist form of life and the place of a critique of capitalism in activism coalescing around 'Black Lives Matter.'

Marx suggests that we think of the form of life as the shape that life takes under certain modes of production. From this perspective, the capitalist form of life is created and reproduced in an attempt to meet needs; it results from the social production of the means of subsistence and from the material activity that is part of social production and the reproduction of life, absorbing the social relations of work in their somatic aspects, and embedding in objects. While it is impossible to separate production and human reproduction, the capitalist form of life dissimulates this impossibility, continually separating the inorganic from the organic, all the better to turn them inside out and conceal them in one another. The aim of Timothée Haug's essay, 'The Capitalist Metabolism,' is to expose this paradoxical mechanism. Haug deploys the metaphor of metabolic processes to revisit Marx's analysis of capitalism as both a mode of production and a form of life, drawing on feminist and ecological criticism. He argues that even as capitalism relies on the reproduction of life (i.e. on non-waged activities, the daily species production performed by women or other gendered workers) it is unable to account for that dependence within the dominant value form. An empirical gap remains among the purchasing and consumptive practices mediating care-work, and these mediations exist within capitalism, but escape commodification.

In the aggregate, the articles in this volume offer a fresh approach to contemporary treatises on how capitalism forms and deforms our lives. Sharon Holland's contribution, 'Vocabularies of Vulnerability,' employs the category of 'forms of life' to address explicitly the connection between human and non-human life, and their respective vulnerabilities. By highlighting issues of language, she also demonstrates that vulnerability appears only insofar as it can exist within a horizon of obligations (irrespective to whether they are fulfilled) and of normative reasoning, and how these constructions are racialized in the United States.

All of the essays – both the short interventions and the longer articles – push capitalism studies to engage with questions that preoccupy scholars of vulnerability. Many theorists today avoid the question of vulnerability, or rush to classify it under the rubric of 'risk.' In doing so they restrict vulnerability to calculations of probability and costs, occluding the ubiquity of vulnerability in the capitalist form of life. Instead we trace the social production of vulnerable lives in their ordinariness, in language, in interactions, and in processes of material sedimentation, as vulnerability persists through the unreflective acceptance of circumstances that are taken as given. We thus invite further investigation into the connection between the defeasibility of the very *forms* of our lives and the vulnerability of *the* human form of life, providing generative possibilities for rethinking and redressing economic precarity as one among other types of vulnerabilities. At the same time, and precisely through this prism, we aim to amplify how forms of life may be critiqued, and thereby wrestled open to needed transformation.

Disclosure statement

No potential conflict of interest was reported by the authors.

References

Adorno, T. (1998). *Critical models*. (H. W. Pickford, Trans.). New York, NY: Columbia University Press.

Adorno, T. (2006). *Minima Moralia*. New York, NY: Verso.

Cavell, S. (1989). *This new yet unapproachable America: Lectures after Emerson after Wittgenstein*. Chicago, IL: University of Chicago Press.

Das, V. (2007). *Life and words. Violence and the descent into the ordinary*. Berkeley: University of California Press.

Jaeggi, R. (2005). No individual can resist: *Minima Moralia* as critique of forms of life. *Constellations, 12*(1), 65–82.

Lukacs G. (1971). *The Theory of the Novel*, trans. Anna Bostock, London: The Merlin Press.

Pitkin, H. (1973). *Wittgenstein and justice: On the significance of Ludwig Wittgenstein for social and political thought*. Berkeley: University of California Press.

Wittengstein, L. (1968). *Philosophical investigations*. (G. E. M. Anscombe, Trans., 3rd ed.). New York, NY: Macmillian.

2 The state of contemporary social philosophy and the tasks of an institute for social research (1931)

Max Horkheimer

Revised translation by Alyson Cole and Estelle Ferrarese*

Although social philosophy is the focus of general philosophical concern, it is in no better shape today than most philosophical, indeed most fundamentally intellectual, efforts. One is unable to find a substantive conception of social philosophy that could be considered everywhere as binding. Given the present situation in the sciences, in which the traditional boundaries between disciplines are in question and we do not yet know where they might be drawn in the future, the attempt to give ultimate definitions for academic domains seems rather untimely. Nevertheless, one can reduce the general views of social philosophy to one brief idea. According to it, the final goal of social philosophy is the philosophical interpretation of human fate – insofar as humans are not mere individuals but members of a community. Social philosophy must therefore primarily concern itself with those phenomena that can be interpreted only in the context of the social life *(Leben)* of humans, such as the state, law, economy, religion; in short, with all of the material and spiritual culture of humanity as such.

Social philosophy, thus understood, became in the history of classical German Idealism the decisive philosophical task. Its most brilliant achievements are in turn the most powerful aspects of Hegel's system. To be sure, even before Hegel, philosophy attempted to understand socio-philosophical phenomena: Kant's main works contain the philosophical theories of science, law, art, and religion. But this kind of social philosophy was grounded in a philosophy of the individual: those realms of being were to be seen as the designs of the autonomous individual. Kant made the total unity of the rational subject into the sole source of all constitutive principles for each cultural sphere. The being and the structure of culture were to be derived solely from the dynamic of the individual, from the basic activities of a spontaneous ego. In terms of Kant's philosophy, we certainly should not equate the autonomous subject with an empirical human being. Nevertheless, we certainly are able to investigate all aspects of cultural creativity in the temperament of each individual rational being. All-encompassing structures of being that belong to a supra-personal whole, and are only discoverable within a social totality to which we would have to subject ourselves, do not

* Original translation by Peter Wagner (*in Critical Theory and Society*, Stephen E. Bronner and Douglas MacKay Kellner ed. , Routledge, 1989), revised translation by Alyson Cole and Estelle Ferrarese.

exist; their assertion would be dogmatic, and any action directed towards them would have to be grounded heteronomically. The moral individual as seen in the *Metaphysical Foundations of Jurisprudence* is thus an individual 'subjected to no other laws than those that it has (either alone or at least together with others) established for itself.'[1]

The German Idealism connected with Kant developed the interconnection between autonomous reason and empirical being. The tension between a finite human being and the ego as infinite obligation can, however, still be discerned – in Fichte's first philosophy of the self-reflecting mind. The eternal ought, the instruction to satisfy our human destiny, flows from the depths of subjectivity. The medium of philosophy is here still self-reflection. But Hegel has freed this self-reflection from the chains of introspection, and referred the question of our own being, the question of the autonomous culture-creating subject, to the labor of history – through which it gives itself objective form.

For Hegel, the structure of objective spirit *(Geist)*, which realizes in history the cultural artifacts of the absolute spirit (i.e. art, religion, philosophy), is not discerned any longer from a critical analysis of personality *(Persönlichkeit)*, but rather from universal dialectical logic. The development and the works of the objective spirit are not arrived at by the free decisions of a subject, but by the spirit of the dominant peoples that succeed each other on the battlefields of history. The destiny of the particular fulfills itself in the fate of the universal. The essence, the substantial content, of the individual is not revealed in personal actions but in the life *(Leben)* of the totality to which it belongs. Thus, Hegel's Idealism has become in its constitutive parts social philosophy: the philosophical understanding of the collective whole, in which we live and which serves as the foundation for all creations of absolute culture, is now simultaneously knowledge of the meaning of our own being, its true worth and contents.

Let me remain for a moment with this Hegelian conception! From its dissolution and the impossibility of recreating it in thought without falling behind the present state of knowledge, one is in principle able to explicate the present state of social philosophy. Hegel assigned the realization of the goal of Reason to the objective spirit, in the last instance to the world-spirit. The development of this spirit is shown in the conflict of the 'concrete ideas,' the 'spirit of the peoples,' out of which 'as signs and ornaments of its grandeur' the world-historical kingdoms emerge in necessary sequence.[2] This development happens regardless of whether individuals in their historical actions know of it and will it; the development has its own law. Nevertheless, as with the French Enlightenment and English Liberalism, Hegel does accept the drives and passions of human beings as real motive powers. Even the great men are driven to their actions by their own ends. They 'have formed purposes to satisfy themselves, not others.'[3] Yet they are in their world, 'its clear-sighted ones; *their* deeds, *their* words are the best of that time.'[4] Nothing, however, has happened in history without 'interest on the part of the actors.'[5] The interests of the great men as well as those of the masses are of course used 'cunningly' by the rational law of development to its own end. And as Hegel explains past history only indirectly with that law, but directly with competing interests, so does he explain the life-process *(Lebenprozess)* of modern society. While himself referring to the liberal economists Smith, Say, and Ricardo, he shows how out of the 'medley of arbitrariness,'[6] which is created by the striving of individuals to satisfy their needs and wants, the totality is maintained. 'In bourgeois society,' he writes in the *Philosophy of Right*, 'each member is his own end, everything else is nothing to him. But except in contact with others he cannot attain the whole compass of his ends, and therefore these others are means to the end of the particular member. A particular end, however, assumes the form of universality through this relation to other people, and it is attained in the simultaneous attainment of the welfare of others.'[7] Thus, and only thus, can the state exist according to Hegel: it is directly determined by the conflict of interest in society.

But if history and the state are created eternally out of the 'medley of arbitrariness,' if therefore the historian has to deal with a chain of pain and death, of stupidity and baseness, and if finite being perishes in indescribable agony and history can be seen in Hegel's term as the 'slaughter-bench at which the happiness of peoples, the wisdom of states, and the virtue of individuals are being sacrificed,'[8] then philosophy transcends the viewpoint of the empirical observer. Because 'what is called reality,' he teaches in the *Philosophy of History*, 'is seen by philosophy only as something rotten, which seems to exist but is not real in and for itself. This insight, one might say, is consolation against the conception of absolute disaster, the madness of all that which has come to pass. Consolation, however, is only a substitute for the misfortune that should never have happened, and makes its home in the finite world. Philosophy is therefore not a consolation; it is more: it reconciles, it transfigures, a reality that appears to be unjust, making it appear rational. It exhibits it as such, shows it to be grounded in the idea itself, as that with which reason is supposed to be satisfied.'[9] The 'transfiguration' of which Hegel speaks is precisely attained by that theory according to which the true essence of human beings does not exist in mere inwardness and the actual fate of finite individuals, but asserts itself in the life *(Leben)* of peoples and is realized in the State. With the thought that the material essence, the idea, is preserved in world history, the destruction of the individual seems to carry no philosophical weight. In this regard, the philosopher is able to declare: 'The particular is for the most part of too trifling value as compared with the general: individuals are sacrificed and abandoned. The idea pays the price of existence and of transitoriness, not from itself, but from the passions of individuals.'[10] Only insofar as the individual partakes in the totality as a living being – or better, only insofar as the totality lives *(lebt)* in the individual – is the individual endowed with reality. For the life *(Leben)* of the totality is the life *(Leben)* of the spirit. The totality at its most determined is the state. It 'does not exist for its citizens; one might say it is the end and they are its means.'[11]

According to Hegel, the finite individual being can attain the conceptual consciousness of its freedom within the state only through idealist speculative thinking. He essentially saw in this mediating function the achievement of his philosophy, and thus of philosophy as such. Philosophy is to him identical with the transfiguration of the real 'that appears unjust.' When the esteem of his system had waned in Germany around the middle of the last century, a future-oriented, individualistic society believing in progress replaced the metaphysics of the objective spirit with an unmediated belief in the prestabilized harmony of individual interests. It seemed as if what was needed to mediate between the empirical existence of the individual and the consciousness of its freedom in the social totality was not philosophy, but steady progress in the positive sciences, technology, and industry. But as the disappointment in that belief grew, a scorned metaphysics took its revenge. Deserted by the philosophical conviction that the divine idea existing within the totality is its true reality, the individual experienced the world as 'medley of arbitrariness' and itself as the mere 'price of existence and transitoriness.' The sober glance directed towards the particular and the immediate was no longer capable of discerning 'the cunning of Reason' behind the surface of warring individual wills, perpetual need, the indignities of the everyday world, and the terror of history. And so Hegel's greatest enemy, Schopenhauer, saw the dawn of his anti-historical, pessimistic, and consolatory philosophy.

The conviction that each and every one by virtue of his association with a historical unity and its own characteristic laws, which forms the dialectic of world history, partakes of the eternal life *(Leben)* of the spirit – this notion ensuring the salvation of the individual from the infamous chain of becoming and perishing – disappeared with objective idealism. The suffering and the death of individuals threatened to appear in their naked meaninglessness – the last fact of an age enthralled by facts. With the deepening of the contradiction in the principle of individualistic form of life *(Lebensform)* (that is the contradiction between the unbroken progress of the happiness of the individuals within a given social context on the one hand and the prospects of their actual situation on the other), philosophy, and especially social philosophy, was called more and more urgently to play the role that Hegel had assigned to it. And social philosophy has heeded that call.

The cautious theory of Marburg neo-Kantianism states that a human being is not just an individual, but a being that stands 'in various pluralities… in rank and file' and that 'only in unity' can fulfill 'the circles of its being,'[12] while the philosophical teachings of the present maintain that the meaning of existence, as in Hegel, fulfills itself only within meta-personal units of history such as class, state, or nation. From Hermann Cohen to Othmar Spann, philosophy has brought forth varying shades of socio-philosophical systems in the last few years. Even recent attempts at grounding moral and legal philosophy anew, in contradistinction to positivism, virtually have only one point in common, namely, the striving to find above and beyond the ground of actual incidents a higher realm of being or, at least, a higher realm of norms or ethics with its own characteristic laws in which finite human beings partake, but which cannot itself be reduced to natural incidences. Indeed, they too form a transition to a new philosophy of an objective spirit. While even Kelsen's individualistic and relativistic theory of law carries these features, one can find them in a higher degree in the formalistic value philosophy of the southwestern neo-Kantian school (as well as in Adolf Reinach's phenomenological theory): the essence of the structures of law – for example, the essence of private property, the essence of promise, the essence of the legal claim – can each be seen in its own 'objective manifestation.' Scheler's material ethics of value, his teaching of the being-in-itself of values, has made recently in the work of its most important representative, Nicolai Hartmann, the conscious connection to the philosophy of the objective spirit. The theory of the spirit of peoples had again been proclaimed by Scheler himself even before the publication of Hartmann's ethics.[13]

All of these projects of contemporary social philosophy seem to provide individual human beings with access into a supra-personal sphere that is more invested with being, more meaningful, more substantial than their own existence. They therefore accomplish the task of transfiguration prescribed by Hegel. Further, in Heidegger's *Sein und Zeit* the only modem philosophical work that radically rejects social philosophy and that discovers real being only in the interior of individually existing human beings – care *(Sorge)* is the focal point. This philosophy of individual human existence is in its simple contents not transfiguration in Hegel's sense. Human existence is in it only a being-unto-death, a sheer finitude. It is a melancholy philosophy. If it is acceptable at this point to put the matter bluntly, one might say that today social philosophy meets the desire of a life *(Leben)* hindered in its own individual pursuit of happiness with a new statement of meaning. Social philosophy appears to be part of the philosophical and religious efforts to plant the hopeless individual existence back into the womb, or to put it, in Sombart's term, in the 'golden ground' of meaningful totalities.

But, ladies and gentlemen, having confronted this situation of social philosophy, let us now turn to delineate its deficiency. Social philosophy today, as we have seen, has taken a generally polemical stand against positivism. Positivism, it is charged, sees only the particular and in the realm of society thus sees only the individual and the relations between individuals; all is exhausted by facts. That there are facts that can be ascertained by means of analytical science, philosophy does not dispute. But philosophy posits against these facts more or less constructively, more or less in its own philosophizing, ideas, essences, totalities, independent spheres of objective spirit, units of meaning, spirit of peoples that it considers to be 'more original' or even 'genuine' elements of being. The discovery of certain unprovable metaphysical presuppositions within positivism is taken by philosophy as constituting lawful ground for raising the metaphysical stakes. So it happens that against the school of Vilfredo Pareto, for example – a school that, because of its positivist understanding of reality, has to deny the existence of class, nation, humanity – various standpoints, from which these entities are posited, are offered as a 'different world view,' a 'different metaphysics,' or a 'different consciousness,' without ever making a binding commitment possible. There are, one might say, different conceptions of reality, which make it possible to investigate what kind of genesis they had, to which sensibility of life *(Lebensgefühl)* and to which social group they belong, without providing an objectively grounded priority.

It is precisely in this dilemma of social philosophy, which speaks of its subject, the cultural life *(Kulturleben)* of humanity, in terms of professions of faith, and which sees the differences between the social theories of Auguste Comte, Karl Marx, Max Weber, and Max Scheler as different acts of faith, rather than distinguishing them in terms of true/false or, as of now, problematic theories – precisely in this dilemma do we perceive the deficiency that has to be overcome. To be sure, the simultaneous existence and validity of varying conceptions of reality signify the contemporary intellectual situation at large, but this variety addresses a plethora of scientific areas and spheres of life *(Lebenssphären)*; it does not concern one and the same conceptual field. The constitutive categories of philology and those of physics might thus diverge so far that it seems difficult to harmonize them; but within physics, indeed within the sciences of inorganic nature in general, there is no such tendency to construct non-compatible concepts of reality; the opposite is rather the case. Here, the concrete scientific investigation of the empirical subject matter proves to be a corrective.

At this point one might interject the view that social philosophy is not a scientific discipline, that it is materialist sociology whose subject matter involves distinct forms of socialization. As a discipline it investigates the various concrete ways in which people live together, all forms of associations: from the family to economic groups, and from political associations to the state and to humanity. In it, one might find objective determinations on the same level as in political economy. But sociology has nothing to say either about the degree of reality or about the value of those phenomena. All that is the province of social philosophy; and for these essential questions as it deals with them there are final pronouncements, but no universally binding, true statements which are an integral part of large-scale investigations.

This view presupposes a conception of philosophy that is no longer tenable. However one might want to draw the boundaries between the particular disciplines of sociology and social philosophy, which, I believe, would necessitate a high degree of arbitrariness, one thing is certain: If socio-philosophical thought about the relationship of the individual to society, the meaning of culture, the formation of communities, or the overall status of social life *(Leben)* – in short, about the great, principal questions – should be left behind as the sediment in the reservoir of social scientific problems, after those problems that can be advanced in concrete investigations have been drained off, then social philosophy can still perform a social function (e.g. that of transfiguration), but its intellectual fruitfulness would be destroyed. The relationship between the philosophical and the empirical disciplines should not be conceptualized as if it were philosophy that treated the essential problems, constructing theories that cannot be attacked by the empirical sciences, its own conceptions of reality and systems embracing the totality, while in contrast empirical science comes out of its long, boring studies fragmented into a thousand individual questions, in order only to end up in the chaos of specialization. This view, according to which the empirical scientist has to regard philosophy as a beautiful yet scientifically fruitless enterprise, and the philosopher in contrast emancipates himself from the empirical scientist because the former assumes that he cannot wait for the latter in his far-reaching quest, is presently being superseded by the thought of an ongoing dialectical permeation and evolution of philosophical theory and empirical-scientific praxis. In this regard, the relations between the philosophy of nature and the natural sciences present us with good examples. Chaotic specialization is not being superseded by bad syntheses of specialized research results, nor is the impartiality of empirical research secured through the attempt to eliminate the theoretical elements with it. Rather, chaotic specialization is overcome by the fact that philosophy is able to inject spiritual impulses into empirical research through its own theoretical intention towards the whole, the essential, while being open enough to be itself influenced and transformed by the developments in concrete research.

The correction of the deficiency in the situation of social philosophy hinted at above seems to us to lie neither in a profession of faith of a more or less constructive interpretation of cultural life, nor in positing a new meaning for society, state, law, and what have you. Today, on the contrary, and I am surely not alone in this opinion, all depends on organizing research around current philosophical problematics which, in turn, philosophers, sociologists, political economists, historians, and psychologists engage by joining enduring research groups in order to do together what in other areas one is able to do alone in the laboratory and what all true scientists have always done: namely, to pursue their philosophical questions directed at the big picture with the finest scientific methods, to transform and to make more precise these questions as the work progresses, to find new methods, and yet never lose sight of the whole. In this way, no positive or negative answers to philosophical questions can be given. Instead, the philosophical questions themselves are dialectically integrated into the empirical scientific process; that is to say, their answers are to be found in the progress of substantive knowledge which also effects the form. This approach to the science of society cannot be mastered by one person alone – given the vast subject matter as well as the variety of indispensable scientific methods whose assistance is called for. Despite the gigantic effort on his part, even Max Scheler has failed in this regard.

…

There is one question around which the discussion of society has started to crystallize itself ever more clearly, in social philosophy, narrowly understood, as well as in the circles of sociology. It is not just a fashionable question, but one which presents an actualized version of some of the most ancient and important philosophical problems; the question of the connection between the economic life *(Leben)* of society, the psychological development of its individuals and the changes within specific areas of culture to which belong not only the intellectual legacy of the sciences, art and religion, but also law, customs, fashion, public opinion, sports, entertainments, lifestyles *(Lebensstil)*, and so on. The intention to study these three processes presents merely an updated version by way of contemporary methodologies and the present state of our knowledge, of the ancient question as to the relation of particular existence and universal reason, of the real and the idea, of life *(Leben)* and spirit – adapted to a new problematic.

Mostly, however, one reflects either metaphysically on the above theme, as in Scheler's 'Sociology of Knowledge,' or one states, more or less dogmatically, some general thesis on it; that is to say, one usually picks one of the theses advanced in history in a simplified fashion and, remaining dogmatically abstract, battles it out with all the other theses. Thus, one can find the following pronouncement: that economy and spirit are the respective expressions of one and the same essence; this amounts to a bad Spinozism. Or one can find the following: ideas, 'spiritual' contents, force themselves into history and determine the actions of humans, so that they become primary while material life *(Leben)* remains merely derivative; world and history have their source in the spirit: this would amount to an abstract, badly understood Hegel. Or one finds the contrary belief: the economy, material being, is the only true reality; the human psyche as well as law, art, and philosophy are purely derivative and mere reflections of it; this would be an abstract and therefore badly understood Marx. Besides the fact that these theses naively posit an uncritical, outdated separation of spirit and reality, a separation that is not dialectically sublated, those kinds of statements, if they are taken seriously in their abstractness, are ultimately devoid of any type of verification procedures: all can indiscriminately claim for themselves to present the truth. These dogmatic convictions are spared the scientific difficulties of the problem, if only because they consciously or unconsciously take the total identity of ideational and material processes for granted – not caring for, or even ignoring, the complex role of the psychic mediations.

The issue is seen quite differently if we pose the question more precisely in the following manner: In a definite time frame and in some particular countries, what relations can we delineate between a particular social group and the role of this group in the economy, the changes in the psychical structure of its members, and the thoughts and institutions created by it which influence it as a whole through the social totality? Then the possibility of real research projects that will be conducted in the Institute can come into view. At first, we would like to direct them towards a very important and particular social group in Germany, skilled labor and white-collar employees, and continue after that with the corresponding segments in the other highly developed European countries.

There is little time left to give a necessarily summary and insufficient overview of the most important paths that the full members of the Institute will have to follow in close-knit fashion to initially gather the empirical material with which the relations in question can be studied. At the top of the list is obviously the interpretation of the published statistics, the reports of organizations and political associations, the material of public corporations, and so on. This can happen only in connection with the ongoing analysis of the overall economic situation. Furthermore, it is necessary to investigate sociologically and psychologically the press and literature for the value of their pronouncements on the situation of the groups in question, but also because of literature's categorical structure, which enables it to influence the members of these groups. Especially important is then the development of a variety of survey methods. Questionnaires, amongst others, can be integrated into our research in manifold ways and can be of good service, if one always keeps in mind that inductive conclusions derived through them alone are always prematurely drawn. The essential purpose of questionnaires in our case is twofold: first, they should stimulate the research and keep it in touch with real life *(Leben)*; second, they can be used to check knowledge gained by other means and thereby preempt errors. For the design of these questionnaires American social research has done important preliminary work which we will assimilate and advance for our own purposes. Also, we will have to use expert opinions on a grander scale. Where it is possible to advance particular aspects of problems by as yet unrecorded experiences of competent evaluators, one should try to include them wherever one might find them. Most times that will mean using the experience of practitioners for the sciences. A special task, moreover, is the collection and interpretation of documents that cannot be found in books. To that end, namely to employ scientifically the extremely rich sociological archives of the International Labor Bureau in Geneva, we will create a branch of the Institute there. Mr. Albert Thomas, the director of the International Labor Organization, has welcomed our plan and assured us, in a most pleasant manner, of his support. One has to add to all these paths, naturally, the methodological study of all published and forthcoming scientific treatises on the subject.

Each of these methods alone is completely insufficient, but perhaps all together, through years of patient and extended research, they might bear fruit for the general problematic. This can only be the case, in turn, if the members of the Institute constantly refer to the material and form their opinions not according to their own preferences, but according to the demands of the subject; if they refrain from all terms of transfiguration – and, finally, if we can preserve the unified intention to oppose both dogmatic ossification and descent into the technical-empirical.

I conclude. It has only been possible for me to delineate from all the tasks of the Institute the collective research work whose implementation will be the focus of the years to come. Besides that, the independent research of the individual members in the areas of theoretical economics, economic history, and the history of the labor movement should equally be borne in mind. The Institute will follow its mandate as a teaching institute within the university by holding regular programs such as lectures, lessons, and talks. These shall be considered additions to the regular university teaching since they will introduce the work of the Institute, report the newest developments in its research, and advance an education that meets the challenge of a philosophically oriented social science as explained above.

I could only hint at all these special tasks. On the other hand, it seems to me as if even this short report about the specifics has weakened our ability to remember the fundamentals. Indeed, this lecture has become almost a symbol for the strange difficulty of social philosophy – that the universal and the particular, the theoretical conceptualization and individual experience, penetrate each other. I am convinced that my explication in this regard has been insufficient. Allowing myself to hope that you have followed this lecture with forbearance, I ask for your good wishes and trust for the work itself. Carl Grunberg talked at the opening of the Institute about the fact that everyone is led in his/her scientific work by the impulse of a worldview. May the guiding impulse of this Institute be the unchangeable will to unflinchingly serve the truth!

Notes

1. Kant, *Sämtliche Werke,* Akademie-Ausgabe, vol. 6, p. 223.
2. Hegel, *Philosophy of Right,* trans. T. R. Knox (London, 1952), par. 352.
3. Hegel, *Philosophy of History,* trans. J. Sibree (New York, 1956), p. 30.
4. Ibid.
5. Ibid., p. 23.
6. Hegel, *Philosophy of Right,* par. 189 Addition.
7. Ibid., par. 182 Addition.
8. Hegel, *Philosophy of History,* p. 21.
9. Hegel, *Philosophie der Weltgeschichte,* ed. G. Lassen (Leipzig, 1920), vol. 1, p. 55.
10. Hegel, *Philosophy of History,* p. 33.
11. Hegel, *Philosophie der Weltgeschichte,* p. 91.
12. Hermann Cohen, *Ethik des reinen Willens* (Ethics of pure will), 3d ed. (Berlin, 1921), p. 8.
13. Max Scheler, 'Probleme einer Soziologie des Wissens,' in Scheler, ed. *Versuche zu einer Soziologie des Wissens* (Munich and Leipzig, 1924), p. 13.

3 Economy as social practice

Rahel Jaeggi

In order to understand the economy in a *wider sense* we should conceive of the economy as a set of social practices. To conceive of a 'practices-oriented' foundation for our thinking about economy and its institutions, we should view economic practices as a subset of social practices in general, sharing the features of 'practices.' As such they are interrelated with other practices in a variety of ways and (together with them) form part of the socio-cultural fabric of society.

To conceive of the economy as a social practice and part of a broader form of life entails:

(1) *First*, the *normativity of economic practices*. The thesis that the market and even economic institutions as such are a 'norm-free sphere' has recently been intensely countered with the argument that economic actors are not free from moral considerations, and even more so, not free from ethical considerations, habits, and dispositions, that is, their 'ethical life' [*Sittlichkeit*]. While agreeing with these diagnoses, my account of the economy as a social practice goes further: Normativity or the ethical background/embeddedness of the economy doesn't come into the picture from the outside, because the economical agents are in fact not free from moral considerations or ethical orientations. If practices are (internally) constituted by norms, then *economic practices also have inherent normative conditions of success*, or ethical-functional norms that are indispensable for their proper functioning.

(2) *Second*, and to very briefly mention Habermas and the differentiation between 'system' and 'lifeworld,' where the capitalist economy belongs to the system, I propose that with a practice-theoretic approach, the alternative between an *action- and a system-theoretic* approach to the economy can be overcome in a meaningful way. One advantage of a systemic view of the economy is that it can grasp 'mechanisms of social integration' that are 'not necessarily intentional, i.e., with communicative effort through the consciousness of participants in interaction, but rather *objectively coordinated* behind their backs, so to speak.' The 'invisible hand' of the market, then, is the paradigmatic case of this sort of regulation. But then: to conceive of the economy as and in a context of social practices doesn't mean that it arises from actions and intentions, or the results of such. Practices are only partially intentional, partially explicit and partially due to the will and actions of people. They are not planned for

in advance, but emerge, and they have habitual elements. When practices 'congeal' into institutions (which I think of as states of aggregate practices), they can achieve their own dynamic and take on a life of their own, a phenomenon that is difficult for the parties involved to see. It might then be fruitful to re-address the 'systemic' phenomena in a practice and institutional theoretical framework, thereby avoiding the unwanted side-effects of an understanding of economics as a non-normative sphere.

(3) *Third*, if it follows from the above-described character of economic activities that, as social practices, they are interrelated with other social practices and aggregate or bundle with them into a form of life, this context must be understood as open. It cannot be clearly or conclusively answered a priori which practices are essential for what purpose and which practices are dependent on each other. We might think of a variety of different relations between these practices, functional dependencies of some sort but also cases in which the relation is looser, mutual, or reciprocal. Even if in some cases one practice is more dominant or 'steers' more than another it shouldn't be taken for granted a priori, for instance, that cultural practices would be premised upon economic practices or vice versa. We might therefore abandon a simplistic 'base/superstructure' model without losing sight of the mutual dependencies between different practices and norms.

(4) *Fourth*: In each of the (only sketched) cases, the extra-economical aspects are not merely *preconditions* for the economical activities and institutions in the narrower or 'proper' sense (i.e., for maximizing utilities in the market, for bringing about results in an instrumental fashion through labor, for being able to divide the world along property- relations). We cannot take these far-reaching preconditions for granted. To conceive of economic attitudes as practices that are interrelated (economic and non-economic) practices, thus as an ensemble within an ensemble, implies that the very distinction between economics and its preconditions, and the inside/outside dichotomy itself turns out to be less informative and less helpful then we previously thought. According to the practice-oriented description of the economic, then, it makes little sense to speak of rescuing a particular class of practices from out of the context of a form of life. Among the basic orientations that we might have to re-examine, then, is the widespread concentration of critical efforts – within critical theory as well as within other discourses critical of capitalism – to *protect* certain spheres (cultural, social, personal) from *contamination* by the supposedly separate economic sphere. Economic practices, according to this view, do not merely rely on or are 'embedded' in a surrounding or enabling ethical form of life; they are rather *part of the form of life* itself and its respective dynamic.

(5) *Fifth*: with a concept of the economic as a nexus of practices we should be able to overcome the narrow concept of the economy famously criticized by Horkheimer in two interrelated ways: *the economy itself* is understood in a wider sense, since it is no longer reduced to the (narrow) attitudes of purpose-oriented utility maximizing behavior that seeks to fulfill narrowly defined interests. But furthermore, the *relation between economic and other social practices* is understood in a wider sense than an economistic determinism allows for.

Does this situatedness of economic practices still hold for capitalist societies? Isn't it a defining feature of a capitalist society that 'the economy' (and economic rationality) has disentangled itself from the web of social practices it was involved in - or, as Polanyi has it: isn't the process of 'disembedding' the economy from its social context the peculiar (and threatening) characteristic of capitalist societies? Capitalism would then not be a 'form of life,' it would not actually 'live' but threaten all forms of life with its dominance (and the domination of abstract and 'dead labor'). In fact, economic practices and institutions in capitalism take on a certain determinate and determining shape, such as private property in the means of production, the existence of a 'free' labor market, and an accumulation of capital oriented toward 'gain' instead of 'need,' i.e. toward the cultivation of more capital instead of the consumption of it or subsistence on it. Economic relations not only overtake other aspects of life, but also develop dynamics of their own that 'exceed the subjective ends and the control of its participants and that, moreover, cannot be affirmed by them collectively.' Here the social is transformed into 'social forces.' This is what we might refer to as the *systemic* character of a capitalist economy. But then, my tentative hypothesis is: The activities involved are still *practices*, based on norms, aggregated into institutions and involved in the larger practical context of a form of life – even if they might turn out to be 'failed practices' in a certain respect. The capitalist organization of the economy only *presents itself* as 'disembedding' or 'de-normativizing', insofar as its dynamic consists in dissolving traditional ethical limits as they expressed themselves institutionally, for example, in premodern guild-like regulations and limitations of economic activity. However, it also constitutes its own, new normativity. I am suggesting here only the absence of *a specific* ethos and the replacement of a norm and its institutional framework *with another one* – one that presents itself as ethically 'neutral' and based on rational preferences and utility maximizing. One should not be fooled by capitalism's tendency to make the normative and the dense ethical character of economic institutions invisible, something that underlies neoclassical economics, for instance. Even the idea of universal exchangeability, as I have suggested, presupposes as well as constitutes a form of life. Even the practice that conceals its 'practice-character' is still a practice. And even dissolving the bonds to other practices is still characterized by entanglements, even if those are based upon 'false abstraction' (from the entanglement with other practices) and working behind our backs, without being (as Hegel might put it) self-consciously embraced. To put it in a manner amenable to Marx's characterization of civil society: the 'context of contextlessness,' ('*Zusammenhang der Zusammenhangslosigkeit*') is still a context. And the ethos of abolishing substantial ethical relations and restrictions, like the ones that were broken in the course of 'modern' or capitalist economic institutions (which are both a presupposition and effect of such relations), is still itself an ethos – the *ethos of capitalism*. But then the *capitalist form of life itself* and its economic practices that comes into view – and the prospect of a debate about and a critique of capitalism *as* a form of life.

I would like to clarify one potential misunderstanding: When I refer to a *critique of capitalism as a form of life*, this should not be equated with the so-called 'ethical critique' of capitalism such as the thematization of the ethically detrimental effects of (what Weber calls) the 'economic mentality' of capitalism or the 'culture of capitalism' on our ways of life. At stake is not critically judging capitalism against a standard of critique based on a theory of the good life. Rather, if economic *practices are conceptualized as practices* within a wider context of practices, as part of the socio-cultural fabric of society, and if even the seemingly inaccessible and self- moving dynamics of economic processes should—in principle—be conceivable as results of a complex chain of practices, what comes into view is rather the prospect of renewing a critique of capitalism as an *irrational* social order in a certain sense.

What, then, is wrong with capitalism (as a form of life)? It is both easy and complicated to explicate what is intrinsically wrong with capitalism. From my discussion at least one *meta-criterion for criticism* evolves that might set the stage for further inquiry. Returning to the matter of 'failed' practices and the supposed ethical neutrality of a capitalist economics: there seems to be something wrong with a social order that relies on an ethics that it at the same times conceals and universalizes as 'neutral.' And there seems to be something wrong with practices that we don't see as practices and that are constituted in such a way that the fact of their artificiality (of their 'being made') is concealed, as is the case with the economic forces that drive our lives in capitalism.

Disclosure statement

No potential conflict of interest was reported by the author.

4 The use of bodies. Agamben's idea of a non-capitalist form of life

Estelle Ferrarese

ABSTRACT
With the notion of the form-of-life as a counter-figure to the notion of bare life, Agamben seems to invite us to place at the center of a critical theory of capitalism a reflection on bios. To envisage a form of emancipation that unfolds against bare life suggests, at first glance, another relation to the living body. Such a gesture seems to be inspired by the desire to think a natural life that would *also* be a politically qualified life. The idea with which Agamben closes the *Homo Sacer* series, namely that of a use of *bodies*, also gestures in this direction. In this paper I show how the categories of bare life and of the use of bodies fail to live up to their promise, before demonstrating in what sense the idea of a subtraction of law as a political project which subsumes all others ends up weakening the critical potential of the idea of a form-of-life that is to be realised against the force of production of bare lives.

Giorgio Agamben's conception of capitalism is limited. One searches his work in vain for a theory of exploitation, of abstract labour, of surplus value, or of the market – even one regulated by the State – or of the commodification of the world. If the influence of Guy Debord often leads Agamben to define our epoch as 'the extreme phase of capitalism,' a phase which is that of the 'spectacle,' he tends to reduce capitalism to the sole phenomenon of commodity fetishism. Since *Stanzas*, he has devoted numerous developments to the spell cast by the appearance of the commodity, and to those phenomena that attribute a quasi-mythical origin and potentiality to certain things which nevertheless arise from a perfectly social logic. In *Profanations*, he even comes to consider capitalism as a religion, an idea which he takes from Benjamin. According to Agamben, capitalism separates each thing from itself by means of the distinction it institutes between use value and exchange value. By doing so – that is, by 'sacralising' things – capitalism extracts them from the sphere of use and transforms them into objects of consumption. Consumption supposes a relation of property over things, with a simultaneous destruction of the thing. In these two respects, it renders use impossible. We will return to this category of use, which lies at the heart of the normative horizon constituted by the form-of-life. For the moment, let us simply note that for Agamben capitalism is a *relation to things and between things*, a relation subsumed under a certain form of political power and which secularises and sediments within it a logic that is above all religious: capitalism 'generalizes in every domain the structure of separation that defines religion' (Agamben, 2007, p. 81).

Moreover, the allusions that Agamben makes to the financial crisis – in interviews, for instance – constitute only an instrumental critique of capitalism. For him, it is not a matter of underscoring the fact that capitalism ceaselessly generates crises in order to then be able to feed off them. The problem for Agamben is that each crisis opens onto a new set of measures, policies and regulations that entrap human beings ever more tightly in *dispositifs* which neutralize all potentiality. Agamben's reasoning is first of all political, in the sense that what he is seeking to denounce is not an economic system but a certain form of political power.

However, the idea of a non-capitalist form-of-life is almost a pleonasm in the conceptual constellation Agamben proposes. A form-of-life is a style of life in which bare life is undistinguished and undistinguishable and bare life characterizes a condition of immediate contact between the body and what destroys it, a condition in which 'power confronts nothing but pure life, without any mediation' (Agamben, 2000, p. 171). In the conditions of modernity, this contact is not contact with the sovereign power itself. Indeed, bare lives are not those facing the firing squad armed by the sovereign, but lives whose destruction cannot be condemned. Bareness is the property of bodies that can be left to the amusements of the camp guard, or can be entrusted to technology and its experiments, or subordinated to the results-driven imperatives of private security companies who wage war in the place of Western armies.

From this perspective capitalism can be analyzed as an ensemble of mechanisms contributing to the production of bare lives, even if Agamben never presents it in this way. In fact, it is easy to demonstrate that the sovereign in his juridical form either does or does not abandon lives to mechanisms that are moved by the growth of value and the extraction of surplus value, for instance by letting the market fix the price of certain medical treatments, by adopting regulations that render probable industrial and ecological catastrophes, by delegating the conditions of incarceration to private enterprises, and so on.

Because the notion of the form-of-life is a counter-figure to the notion of bare life, and because capitalism is one of the forces producing, exploiting and letting die bare lives, Agamben seems to invite us to place at the centre of a critical theory of capitalism a reflection on bios. To envisage a form of emancipation that unfolds against bare life suggests, at first glance, another relation to the living body. Such a gesture seems to be inspired by the desire to think a natural life, which would *also* be a politically 'qualified' life, and not only *zoê*. The idea with which Agamben closes the *Homo Sacer* series, namely that of a use of *bodies*, also seems to gesture in this direction. We will examine the first, then the second, and show how the categories of bare life and the use of bodies fail to live up to their promise, before demonstrating in what sense the idea of a subtraction of law as a political project which subsumes all others ends up weakening the critical potential of the idea of a form-of-life that is to be realised against the force of production of bare lives.

1. Omnipresent yet untraceable bodies

While he gives it no precise content, Agamben nevertheless adorns the reality of a form-of-life with a plurality of effects. It first upholds indeterminacy and makes possible the emergence of a power: a life that cannot be separated from its form is a life 'in which the single ways, acts, and processes of living are never simply *facts* but always and above all *possibilities* of life, always and above all *power*' (Agamben, 2000, p. 4). It also allows for the search for happiness, and for the emergence of a being-in-common. If bare life is life that has been separated from its form, one might expect it to be defined as a life stripped of all the elements, that it would be defined as a non-qualified life. This is indeed the case, but only partially so. These themes are not listed in order to describe what a life deprived of them would look like. And, conversely, no possible articulation of the living body, of potentiality and of the search for happiness can be envisaged on the basis of Agamben's work.

Bare life, or life separated from its form, is defined in three ways: (1) by its unintelligibility, (2) by the fact that existence is reduced to a state of survival, and (3) by an unlimited exposure to injury and murder, which in this case do not count as crimes. In reality, it is this final aspect that Agamben focuses on, shifting the problem of a life stripped of its form from non-qualification to physical vulnerability.

(1) Bare life is distinguished by its ineffability and impenetrability. Bare life is mute, undifferentiated, and devoid of both the generality and particularity that language makes possible (Wall, 2005, p. 41). Nothing therefore seems to distinguish bare life from simple biological life. In an Arendtian vein, the vulnerable body concerns that which is given, that which is immediate yet never elaborated, and that which allows no form of transcendence: a life closed in on itself.

(2) The concept of bare life is associated with *needy and excluded bodies*, that is, bodies that are bound to suffering and forced into mere subsistence (Agamben, 2000, p. 30).

We could find here a critique of labour, that is, of the extortion of labour, or of a certain form of the organisation of labour that lies at the heart of capitalism – a form that crushes certain bodies and keeps others far from any labour, thus transforming them into waste products. But Agamben never elaborates such a critique. Once again, he is dealing with biological life, and the body is never thematized here except in terms of its subjugation to vital processes; its being enchained to the repetitiveness of their rhythms.

(3) And yet bare life is defined first and foremost by its exposure. Here, Agamben radicalizes and de-historicizes Foucault's famous postulate that sovereignty is characterized by the right to take life or to let life continue by arguing that the production of bare lives, that is, of killable bodies, is the original act of sovereign power. The sovereign is he who decides on bareness, Agamben seems to say. The secret substratum of power is therefore the body of subjects: political power 'is not founded – in the last instance – on a political will but rather on bare life, which is kept safe and protected only to the degree to which it submits itself to the sovereign's (or the law's) right of life and death' (Agamben, 2000, p. 5).

As we have indicated above, with modernity, exposure is transformed into a second vulnerability, direct physical destruction being made possible by political indifference, by abandonment by the sovereign power. In any case, in Agamben's work it is the condition of an exposure at each moment to the threat of death that is the means of radical exclusion, the sign of the denial of all justice – both human and divine – and the mark of the withdrawal of all value from this life.

This pre-eminence of the motif of destructibility over the other dimensions of bare life raises a number of difficulties. First, by bringing together under the same expression both biological life and the life that is at the perpetual mercy of blows and of murder, Agamben himself questions what he otherwise insists on, namely, that bare life is not something that exists before its relation to the sovereign. He frequently points out the fact that

> there is not *first* life as a natural biological given and anomie as the state of nature, and *then* their implication in law through the state of exception. On the contrary, the very possibility of distinguishing life and law, anomy and nomos, coincides with their articulation in the biopolitical machine. (Agamben, 2005, p. 87)

Bare life therefore seems to be a product of the machine and not something that exists prior. It is difficult to reconcile this with the accent that is elsewhere placed, via the idea of bare life, on a life closed in upon itself and riveted to its bodily rhythms, that is, upon biological life.

Another problem stems from the gesture of reducing a life deprived of 'form' to a life exposed to murder and to injury— a problem that is above all normative in nature. What is the political horizon suggested by the concept of form-of-life that Agamben carves out? To the extent that the prevalence of the motif of bare life commits us to interpreting the impossibility of a separation between form and life as the impossibility of a decision that would expose someone to murder, we can draw two different normative consequences. Either the form-of-life is conceived as a form that simply protects life; or the form-of-life refers to the good life and includes – in a mode that does not simply make them mere side effects —power and being-in-common. But then, the question of the link between the possibility of indeterminacy and of being-together on the one hand, and the impossibility of murder on the other hand, must be addressed.

The first interpretation seems to invite us to think of the protection of life without recourse to the figure of the sovereign, in the manner of a horizontal pact, or of a social contract without submission to the authority of a *dominus*. If Agamben devotes a few pages of *The Highest Poverty* to the 'constitutive act' represented by the creation of a monastery that gives itself a rule, to its character of a '*pactum*,' it can be doubted whether, with respect to Agamben's main political references, from Walter Benjamin to Guy Debord, the political project attached to this self-organization is limited to the Hobbesian preoccupation with the accommodation of interests to the survival of each person. But how, precisely, are forms-of-life and forms of (bodily) security intertwined? In what sense could lives led in forms-of-life devoid of sovereignty lose their vulnerability?

Above all, such a project of a form-of-life seems to be undergirded by the phantasm of a style of life in which it becomes possible to forget the body; which would efface itself as soon as the problem of its essential fragility becomes less urgent. Yet this offers no perspective from which to think a new relation to the living body.

If we choose the second interpretation, which involves associating, on the one hand, non-qualification of life with the absence of protection, and on the other hand qualification and protection, it must be noted that Agamben does not clarify the reason for which a threat to survival reveals itself to be a threat to the good life. It is doubtful whether political indifference really always deprives the ensemble of those who are affected by it of the attributes of the form-of-life, such as those of power and being-together. On the contrary, is the possibility of murder truly the only – or even the main – obstacle to the deployment of power, to the maintenance of indeterminacy? We can only point out here in Agamben's framework the breathtaking retrocession to the status of theoretical backdrop of such phenomena as (the most humble) poverty, brutal inequalities, and forms of domination whose domain is not that of the body, which vanish behind the suspension of survival by political decision. For indeed, in what sense would a life whose maintenance was not left to the amusement of the guardian or to the arbitrary decision of the doctor be a life of power? A life that cannot be separated from its form is a life whose possibilities are not completely exhausted or extinguished; in which it is still possible to do or not to do, to succeed or to fail. A life shackled – not biologically but indeed socially – to specific tasks or a determinate identity can be a life just as deprived of possibilities as a life in the hands of guardians or experts.

In any case, the body that lies, in its essential fragility, at the centre of the idea of bare life seems to vanish as soon as it is a matter of envisaging a qualified life. Agamben offers us nothing with which to think the link between the non-exposed body and potentiality (for example, nothing permits us to think that Agamben would attach a form of conatus to this body), nor the link between a life indistinguishable from its form and its search for happiness (to name one theoretical option among others, Agamben does not seem to be thinking of an organisation of existence around eroticism). In the most conventional manner possible in political theory, the vulnerability of the human body is only visible for the time it takes to neutralize it, without opening up any new perspectives. Another way seems to be possible for thinking the living body and form-of-life, with the idea of the use of bodies that Agamben has recently developed.

2. The use of bodies

It is to this theme, which was already heralded in his previous works, especially *The Highest Poverty*, that Agamben devotes the work that concludes the *Homo Sacer* series – a fact that seems to confer upon it a cardinal importance in terms of the question of determining what a life that cannot be separated from its form is. To make *use* of the model of a shared relation to the world, is to *realize a form-of-life*. The idea of use, in its double incompatibility with property and exchange, seems moreover to be particularly pertinent, a priori, for establishing the conditions of an escape from the capitalist life.

Once again, as for the majority of the categories that he employs, Agamben proceeds by accumulation – by the superposition of definitions – in order to give an idea consistency. But this superposition is not without its incoherencies.

(1) Use seems to designate a human activity that can be reduced neither to production (it does not manifest itself by the realization of work) nor to praxis (acting well is not in itself the end). It constitutes a continuous practice. Supposing no implementation, it invents itself step by step. With the idea of use, human activity is displaced from the level of practice and action towards the way of living. It is a matter of envisaging, in a manner akin to Wittgenstein, a use which exists only as a sort of limit point at which 'explanations and justifications seem to stop' (Agamben, 2016, p. 240). Using things and bodies is preceded by no project, principle or intention that would be applied or put to 'work.' Use is not putting knowledge into practice, and rests on no instrumental faculty.

The very idea of will as a characteristic of the human being has to be dissolved into this category of use, for it is nothing other than an apparatus that embeds human life within a regime of responsibility and dispossession. Agamben finds in Saint Francis of Assisi the proposition of a *forma vivendi* in which 'life […] maintains itself in relation, not only to things, but even to itself in the mode of inappropriability and of the refusal of the very idea of a will of one's own' (Agamben, 2013, p. 140). With it, Agamben is convinced that he has encapsulated a new figure of the human act that allows us to decenter 'action' as a fundamental concept of politics.

(2) Use is a category that is irreducible to the duality of potentiality and the act. Agamben seeks to think a potentiality within the act, but also a potentiality that is such that it is within its own potential *not* to be. His aim is to give a consistency to the idea of a potentiality which is not opposed to impotence, but which is like a potentiality-in-act which affirms itself on the very basis of the fact of its impotence: 'Use is, in this sense, a principle internal to potential, which prevents it from being simply consumed in the act' (Agamben, 2016, p. 93). Use does not 'end' in a work; rather, such a work is deactivated and rendered inoperative, returned to possibility and opened to a new possible use.

These two elements of the definition, namely use as an alternative to action and use as never exhausting potentiality seem to make the category of use the basis of a critical figure of the Subject, of its predicates and of its relation to the world.

(3) Use is opposed to possession and above all to property. To make use of something therefore comes down to not appropriating something. As early as *Means Without Ends*, Agamben had stated: 'we call common the point of indifference between the proper and the improper, that is, something which cannot be grasped in terms of appropriation or expropriation but only as use' (Agamben, 2000, p. 117).

This aspect of use could also be the basis for a critical theory of the subject inasmuch as it brings with it a theory of the object as neither constituted by the subject nor as simply available to the subject. Moreover, from the perspective of a critique of capitalism, such considerations could lead to the evocation of a form-of-life in which the labour force of each person would no longer be their private property. Henceforth one could no longer 'freely' sell their labour; on the contrary, the community would make use of it. Following Marx, we can consider part of the problem of exploitation to reside in the dispositif of the possession of the labor force. Now, the illusion of the freedom of selling one's labour has as much to do with the juridical apparatus which frames the contract, as it does with the fiction that defines the parties to the contract that the contract supposes. Since the individual is conceived as the proprietor of their own person, of their own attributes and qualities, they can choose to give up some in exchange for other goods or services.

But a new chiasm now emerges here in Agamben's reasoning, which cuts off the possibility of this interpretation. Agamben makes clear that inappropriability is not a decision, but rather a state of the world. Use is a relation to the inappropriable. The list of examples mobilised by Agamben to illustrate what the inappropriable is, from the landscape to language and the body, makes the inappropriable a simple *attribute* of things, and not a human organisation of things. Thus, as far as the body is concerned, the inappropriable refers to the ontological phenomenon of the inappropriability of my own body by myself: 'My body is given to me originarily as the most proper thing, only to the extent to which it reveals itself to be absolutely inappropriable' (Agamben, 2016, p. 85), in particular when it is subject to imperious needs. The problem that Agamben circumscribes is therefore less of a political than of a cognitive order: if consumers are unhappy in mass societies it is above all because they *believe* that they exert over the objects they consume their right to property, and are thus unaware of their ontological inappropriability. The impossibility of use at the heart of capitalism would therefore result, more so than from a logic of means of production, of the accumulation of value and of domination which divides the world between a limited number of owners, than from a shared error regarding the nature of things – things which, in reality, *cannot* be possessed. Against Agamben's approach it is necessary to recall that history is a history of the endless development of the commodification of the world and the atrophy of the commons, and has demonstrated in every imaginable way that inappropriability is neither a state of the world nor a characteristic of the object in itself, whether this object be the human body and its organs or the environment - which is distributed even before being known. Inappropriability is not something that must be recognised through an effort of lucidity; it must be established and guaranteed politically.

The category of use therefore constitutes a problem in itself, and the difficulty only grows as soon as we apprehend it in relation to the human body. There is a very strong link between use and the body in the conceptual constellation Agamben establishes, a link that is not limited to merely applying the category of use, as a general form of the relation to things, to a particular thing, namely the body. In *Profanations*, when he endeavours to define an unprofanable – that is, something that would be impossible to extract from the sacred in order to restore it to use – Agamben finds it in pornography. The latter is supposed to have 'realised the capitalist dream of the production of the Unprofanable' (Agamben, 2007, 89). It neutralises the human capacity to make erotic behaviours turn about in the void, that is, to profane them by detaching them from their immediate finality. If capitalism prevents use, it is with pornography and the organisation it imposes upon bodies that use is definitively neutralised. The body is therefore the motif that allows us to grasp fully what Agamben has in mind when he envisages the generalisation of use as a path for the realisation of a form-of-life.

In the work which he devotes to this theme, the introduction to the category of the use of bodies occurs by way of the figure of the slave and its definition by Aristotle as 'the being whose work is the use of the body' (Agamben, 2016, p. 10), a figure who would allow us to circumscribe an 'other' way of being human. Obviously, Agamben does not seek to generalize the juridical reality of the slave in the Greek and Roman worlds. Rather, slavery represents 'the parodic realization within social institutions' of this 'use of the body,' of a body that is the bearer of a different kind of act – an act which Agamben is here seeking to define. But it is not certain that this category can be extracted without remainder from its origin in a very particular institution, i.e. slavery. The idea of use also refers to the fact that the slave is part of the body of the master – a fact that Agamben will reinscribe, in a somewhat troublesome manner from the point of view of gender, through the following formula: 'the use of the body defines a zone of indifference between one's own body and the body of another' (Agamben, 2016, p. 22). In fact, the expression 'use of bodies' is employed throughout the book in order to refer to situations that indifferently involve one's own body and the bodies of others. The one *and* the other have the same characteristics of non-instrumental activity, of an activity without the production of a work; an activity governed by no knowledge and which never exhausts its power.

In his attempt to get rid of the idea of action, Agamben insists on the fact that the concept of use blurs the boundary between agent and patient. He notably defends the idea that contemplation is the paradigm of use, insofar as its practice dissolves the subject just as it dissolves the object (Agamben, 2016, p. 63). The first abandons itself to it, or loses itself in it, while the second is never constituted as such since the contemplator only ever contemplates their own potentiality.

From this perspective, Agamben, following Foucault, also draws on the model of sadomasochism. According to him, S&M reveals the truth of use by bringing to light the activity that is included in passivity, that is, the indistinguishability between these two moments inasmuch as one of the two partners makes themselves be and do something for the other. Furthermore, the use of the body expresses the affect one receives insofar as one is in relation to other bodies. In order to enter into a relation of use with something I must be affected by it, that is, I must constitute myself as the person who is making use of it. Agamben adds that 'in the using of something, it is the very being of the one using that is first of all at stake' (2016, p. 30). Thus, far from proffering a critique of the 'availability' and the disposability of the body, the concept of 'use' describes an indistinction between agent and patient in order to rethink the figure of the subject – a subject from whom only intention and work have been subtracted. There is much to be said for this, but the question of the power of this subject purified of its traditional predicates is not posed. Here, Agamben ultimately falls back into a mode of thinking that he himself disavows, and seems to consider power as a matter only of intention and will – in short, as an attribute of a subject – and thus omits the weight both of structures and of History. With the traditional figure of the subject now dissolved, there is supposed to remain only relations that are both egalitarian and without constraint.

The apparatus of a subject who has a will, a rationality who is the proprietor of themselves no doubt merits its own deactivation; but from the point of view of feminised subjects, a common use of bodies is very close to bare life, that is, to lives that are at the mercy of a decision, whether this decision be a matter of sexuality or of procreation. And whether or not the form of the will is replaced, along with the idea of use, with habit or with invention that proceeds step by step, this changes nothing for the body in question. The very curious idea of inappropriability that Agamben sets up seeks the political salvation of the *user* – their liberation from the apparatus of the subject – and not of the *used*. Yet very often these positions are not reversible.

If Agamben recognizes perfectly well in passing that the relation of use can 'be degraded to the level of exploitation' (Agamben, 2016, p. 14) – it seems to us that the task of a normative theory of the form-of-life which is defined by use is precisely to determine the threshold and the social conditions of its crossing, as well as the political responses to this exposure.

The problem becomes even more pressing since use cannot be framed in juridical terms. In Agamben's work, we find a refusal of all constituted power; for him, it is indeed a matter of dethroning law once and for all.

3. Lives extricated from law

In *The Highest Poverty*, monasticism – at least in the form that early Franciscanism took in its conflict with the curia between 1279 and 1322 – is interpreted as an attempt to realize a form-of-life. The only example of a form-of-life that Agamben discusses in his work is therefore an unlikely and pre-modern one. More fundamentally, it earns this distinction because Franciscanism, so Agamben claims, tried to imagine a human life entirely removed from the grasp of the law. As Agamben states: 'We call this life that is unattainable by law "form-of-life".' (Agamben, 2013, p. 111)

Agamben attempts to establish in a number of different ways the non-juridical nature of the texts which indicate the rules the different monastic orders gave themselves (for example, by mobilizing the argument according to which these rules did not envisage particular acts but rather outlined a norm that referred to existence in its entirety; or else by showing that their jurisdiction was not of the order of a sanction). If he evokes the habits and temporal scansions that bind the bodies of the monks as apparatuses that render rule and life indiscernible, it is not from their process-like nature that the form-of-life emerges. The rule figures in this essay on the form-of-life not insofar as it is a mechanism for the *incarnation* (of ideals), but insofar as it *is not* the law. It is in this way, more so than by a new relation to the living body, that Agamben defines this example without precedent and without successor as a form-of-life: 'Franciscanism can be defined – and in this consists its novelty, even today unthought, and in the present conditions of society, totally unthinkable – as the attempt to realize a human life and practice absolutely outside the determinations of the law' (Agamben, 2013, p. 110).

According to Agamben, the Franciscan escapes from the law by virtue of two distinct logics.

(1) He describes monastic rules as 'constitutive': they produce conduct by creating the monk's life. Rules and life cannot be distinguished from one another: the 'form-of-life' corresponds to 'the collection of constitutive rules that define it' (Agamben, 2013, p. 71) *at the same time as it creates* the rules. Agamben refers to Wittgenstein's concept of 'constitutive norms' and the example of chess pawns: 'Can one say in this sense that the monk, like the pawn in chess, is defined by the sum of the prescriptions according to which he lives?' he asks (Agamben, 2013, p. 71), to then answer with a correction: could we not say with as much truth that it is the monk's form-of-life that creates the rules? The suggested solution is therefore to remain in a zone of indifference. By promising to observe the rules and life of Saint Francis, a monk is not obliging himself to observe specific norms or the three main vows, but to obey all of these things indiscriminately. The friar minor does not obey rules, but rather 'lives' in obedience. The life of Christ is the rule. It is not about applying a law, formalized principles or a more or less coherent system of ideas and doctrines to life. The Franciscans thereby free themselves from the *form* of law.

(2) Furthermore, according to Agamben the monks put into practice a type of renunciation of property that was both individual and collective, and which puts them out of reach of the law understood as a regime of appropriation. In exchange for their renunciation of real rights (the right to possess, to bring legal action, to inherit, etc.), the friar minors claim to practice a 'moderate use' of material goods (according to the Franciscan definition *usus pauper*, or poor use) and develop the concept of the 'simple use of necessities' (*simplex usus facti*). While it implies moderation and restraint, it is justified only on the basis of the *state of necessity*, as dictated by hunger, fatigue or cold.

It is therefore because they claimed a particular form of use that the Franciscans realised a form-of-life. This implies that use *as such* is a mode of extraction from law, and not its result: it is a mode of subtraction from the system of power which law organizes, namely sovereignty, and at the same time from bare life. Use and law are incompatible because the relations to bodies they bring with them cannot be reconciled.

The Franciscans would therefore have freed themselves from the relation to things and to themselves that the law presupposes and reproduces in its capacity as the foundation of property. But this thematic of the intrinsic link between law and appropriation is not dealt with in a strictly Marxist vein. The principal problem is not that bourgeois law permits and dissimulates a process of endless valorization from which the proprietors of the means of production benefit, and which guarantees their dominion over workers. It is that law itself snuffs out any potentiality, fixing lives to social identities. It is that law is deployed via the apparatus of the Subject or leads ultimately to hiding the truly inappropriable nature of things from us.

The political genesis of the form-of-life must therefore proceed from suspension, secession, subtraction. In other words, Agamben outlines a life actively placed outside of political order. The 'anarchist' project of a form-of-life that rests on a permanent destitution – in opposition to the classical motif at the heart of the political theory of constitutive power – results from a conception of law borrowed from Walter Benjamin as being founded on violence. This permanent deactivation of law and de-institutionalization is thought as a means of 'rendering destitute all juridical and social ownership, without this deposition founding a new identity' (Agamben, 2013, p. 274). Such a project supposes beyond any doubt a resolutely optimistic anthropology and a disconcerting explanatory monism. Only law can expose us to death. And following the theoretical slippage that we have identified in the first part of this article, only law would expose us to impotence.

But are there not a multitude of other radical forms of exposure – to the violence of a partner or of a pimp, to the goodwill of an employer or of the person on whom I am economically dependent, to models of cultural values that constitute me as a subject who is radically inferior to others, to speech acts, all of which are forms of exposure that will survive without any difficulty the abolition of this law?

Still, one might imagine that the renunciation of the world undertaken by the Franciscans would be the starting point for Agamben for a new attention to the precarious life, and the specific needs of the body. 'It is not the rule so much as the state of necessity that is the apparatus through which they seek to neutralize law', Agamben states for example (2013, p.116). But this path is not explored any further; even following this reasoning, Agamben does not speak of life as a set of vital processes. The form-of-life is not a form that would accommodate the body insofar as it is disabled, pregnant, ageing or starving.

In contradiction with this approach to life as an experience of lack, we also find, in the same work, a brief definition of life as a unique substance distributed across a plurality of forms, and which is the bearer of a vegetative, indeed contemplative logic, such as it appears in Plotinus. But it also emerges as a flux of passions: one of the very rare passages in which bodily processes appear as such deals with sexual life, such as it is presented in the sexual biographies compiled by Krafft-Ebing in *Psychopathia sexualis*. It is a matter here of a life that has nothing contemplative nor necessary about it. In sum, Agamben's 'life' is so stripped of concreteness that it gives us no indication as to what the impossibility to distinguish it from its form would mean for us.

It therefore appears that, in terms of the double description of the extraction of life from the prison of law – that is, by the rule and by a use practiced according to needs – only the first constitutes a complete argument. The second, for lack of coherence, neglects what the 'life' which is to be disincarnated is. Agamben thus implicitly redefines the 'life' of the form-of-life as existence, which it is in the first description. He thereby eliminates the bodies and the needs whose non-respect nevertheless constituted the matrix of his critique of sovereignty. More broadly, then, and despite appearances, the incarnated – and therefore also the sexed – nature of the political subject thus remains on the borders of Agamben's political project.

An attentive reading of Agamben's work thus brings to light bodies that are omnipresent in their exposure to death but deprived of qualities capable of giving a content to the promises of the idea of the form-of-life: that is, to the project of a life which is impossible to distinguish from its form. It also illuminates a category of use that is mobilised against the idea of property, but which is extracted in order to think, first of all, a relation to the body without any distinction between one's own body and the body of the other, regardless of the possibility of the impotence to which the body of the other is assigned. Finally, it describes lives that it would be necessary to extract not so from the market and from labour but rather so from law – lives whose very materiality is fragile.

At the same time, by its weaknesses, Agamben's theory invites us to formulate a critique of the capitalist form of life from the point of view of the living body – a critique whose point of departure would be a body exposed to a multiplicity of risks and of torts, which intersect and are stratified into inequality and oppression. It engages us in thinking the threshold between use and exploitation, which implies that we cease to apprehend exploitation from the exclusive perspective of surplus value and therefore of the salariat. Finally, it calls us to grasp the political subject as it is constituted by the experience of lack, of incompleteness and of dependence, rather than by a will or a knowledge.

Disclosure statement

No potential conflict of interest was reported by the author.

References

Agamben, G. (2000). *Means without ends. Notes of politics*. (C. Casarino and V. Binetti, Trans.). Minneapolis: Minnesota University Press.

Agamben, G. (2005). *State of exception*. (K. Fort, Trans.). Chicago: The University of Chicago Press.

Agamben, G. (2007). *Profanations*. (J. Fort, Trans.). New York: Zone Books.

Agamben, G. (2013). *The highest poverty: Monastic rules and form-of-life*. (A. Kotsko, Trans.). Stanford: Stanford University Press.

Agamben, G. (2016). *The use of bodies*. (A. Kotsko, Trans.). Stanford: Stanford University Press.

Wall, Th C. (2005). Au Hasard. In A. Norris (Ed.), *Politics, metaphysics and death: Essays on Giorgio Agamben's Homo Sacer* (pp. 31–48). Durham: Duke University Press.

5 Universal alienation

David Harvey

ABSTRACT
The evidence of alienation with respect to work, daily life, politics and inclusion is widespread and has much to do with the increasing influence of right wing populism. Marx changed the basis for his thinking about alienation from a subjective humanist to an objective historical materialist basis. But the relations between the two forms of alienation cannot easily be severed. The contemporary conditions producing subjective states of alienation need to be investigated, chief among these is the rise of personal indebtedness that forecloses upon future possibilities and restricts freedoms. Debt peonage and alienation are in our times a primary material basis for increasing subjective states of alienation.

In *Seventeen Contradictions and the End of Capitalism* title I identify three main threats to the future of global capitalism (Harvey, 2014). The first is the deteriorating relation to nature. The second is compound growth (endless accumulation of capital) at three percent forever. And the third is universal alienation. This last condition, strongly associated with the first two, typically produces increasingly problematic political and geopolitical instability both within and across the state system. The most obvious manifestation of this is the rise of right wing nationalist parties and authoritarian populism around the world. Universal alienation also underpins many a personal tragedy, such as that of the opioid epidemic along with deaths from chronic alcoholism in many 'forgotten' parts of the United States (where life expectancy is, as a result, on the decline). It also is reflected in the suicides of rice farmers in South Korea of peasant cultivators in India, among hill farmers in Britain, Foxconn workers in Shenzhen and unemployed but foreclosed upon homeowners in Greece, just to cite a few examples. So how are we to interpret universal alienation and from whence does it come?

'Universal alienation' is a concept that has a troubled if not peculiar history in Marx's thought (Mesjaros, 1970). While alienation is prominent in his early works, such as *The Economic and Philosophic Manuscripts of 1844*, it disappears in the late 1840s as Marx explores principles of historical materialism (e.g. in *The German Ideology*) only to reappear as a central conception in the *Grundrisse* (1857). It then seemingly fades into the background of *Capital* (first volume published in 1867) and disappears almost entirely in his later works and notebooks.

Most subsequent critical attempts to resurrect the concept have focused on Marx's early works. Little attention is paid to the radical reformulation of the concept in the *Grundrisse*. Zhang's (2014, p. 481) reconstruction is a significant exception. The 'scientific' presentation of the concept in the *Grundrisse* was, he writes,

> fundamentally different from his past use of the humanist alienation conception … In fact, these were two completely different conceptions of alienation; the labor alienation in the *1844 Manuscript* was a humanist value postulate; the idealized essence that it formed was at odds with reality. This was a contradiction between **imaginary** and **real** … The self-alienation of labor was a logical reflection, established in ideas … The labor alienation in *Grundrisse*, on the other hand, was fundamentally Marx's reflection on real history. The objectified results of workers' past labor actually became the rulers and exploiters of today's workers. The 'past' created by workers becomes the ruler of the 'present' … Hired labor necessarily created a ruling power transformed out of itself: capital. This is the actual alienation of capital and labor relations that Marx describes.

The *Grundrisse* reformulates the concept of alienation through the application of the techniques of historical materialism to the subject matter of *The Economic and Philosophic Manuscripts*. Subsequent attempts, such as that of Jaeggi (2014, p. 32), to reconstruct the ideals of self-alienation as set out in Marx's early work have had to surmount objections to the 'essentialism and perfectionism' assumed in the humanist concept of species being. Is it possible, Jaeggi asks, 'to avail ourselves of the critical import of the concept of alienation without relying on the certainty of a final harmony or reconciliation, on the idea of a fully transparent individual, or on the illusion of having oneself and the world completely at one's disposal or command'. While she answers this question in the affirmative, she does so by ignoring the revolutionary reformulation that occurs in Marx's *Grundrisse*. The revolution laid out in the *Grundrisse* was not so much an epistemological break as a radical reformulation. The humanism of the early Marx (particularly when re-cast in the manner that Jaeggi proposes) can be re-rooted and reconceptualized in the scientific mode proposed in the *Grundrisse*. To some degree such a reconciliation is implicit in Ollman's (1972) work, where Marx's value theory is understood as a theory of alienated labour. This was also my intention in resurrecting the concept of 'revolutionary humanism' in the conclusion to *Seventeen Contradictions*.

So what then, would 'universal' alienation mean in the light of these contrasting formulations? In the early Marx the universality is rooted in the supposed inherent qualities of our species being. The potentiality for realising those qualities is frustrated by capital. The labourers who produce capital are denied the fruits of their labour (they stand in a relation of alienation to their product, the value they produce and to the labour process in which they engage). The individual potential to achieve self-perfection (in social relations, in the relation to nature and in the experience of the labour process) is denied. The advantage of such a formulation is that it is forward looking and aspirational. The sensual and existential experiences evoked in the early works remain important issues. The alienation of labour from the product, from its value and from the design of its production is common to *The Economic and Philosophic Manuscripts* and *Capital*. But in the early works the understanding is not rooted in the realities of the daily life and labors of the workers.

In the *Grundrisse*, the universality of alienation arises out of the historical tendency within capital to create the world market, to establish its social (class) and metabolic relations everywhere and to inscribe certain identifiable laws of motion into human history under the rule of the coercive laws of competition. The 'universality' is specific to capitalism's historical evolution. The problem from the *Grundrisse* onwards into *Capital* is to identify the laws of motion of capital and to understand how these laws govern the conditions of daily life and labour for the mass of the working population. The political project is to liberate ourselves, in thought as well as in political and economic practices, from the constraints imposed by these laws of value and of motion.

Alienation is not confined to labour. In *Capital* we see that the capitalist is compelled by the coercive laws of competition to (a) increase the length of the working day to its maximum no matter what; (b) to reinvest the surplus rather than to indulge in consumer pleasures; (c) to procure relative surplus value through seeking out and adopting new technologies; (d) to produce increasing social inequality and an industrial reserve army; and much more. These are not free choices for the capitalists. The coercive laws of competition force them to extend the working day and intensify the labour process irrespective of their good or ill will. Capitalists have then to excuse, legitimize or simply live with their own barbaric practices . The persona of many capitalists is profoundly shaped by the practices they have to perform. Unsurprisingly, many acquire a sadistic streak. Others become narcissists believing they have a God-given right to create a world in their own image no matter what the consequences for those they employ. Their wealth and well-being is essential, they suppose, to the wealth and well-being of society. Objective conditions have subjective consequences (Zhang, 2011).

The contradictions of alienation

The verb to alienate has various meanings. Legally, it means to transfer a property right to the ownership of another. I alienate a piece of land when I sell it or relinquish the right to use it to another. Exchange always involves alienation (Harvey, 2014, p. 267). Workers alienate their labour power when they enter the factory to do whatever the capitalist commands. But alienation also entails the loss of trust, fairness or reciprocity. Workers 'freely' give of their labour but do so under conditions of coercion or consent that ensure the value they produce is not returned to them but appropriated by capital. The exchange is legal but there is something fraudulent about it. The capitalist appropriates the intelligence and skills of the worker, the capacities for cooperation, initiative and innovation and gives only the value of labour power as a commodity in return. Capitalists have to do this, given the coercive laws of competition. For the labourers, the response is a sense of loss and unfairness, of powerlessness and loss of dignity, which is prone to provoke resentment, anger and frustration. Capital produces alienation in both its objective and subjective garbs.

When Marx was writing capitalist social relations and the laws of motion dominated in only a relatively small corner of the world (Britain, Western Europe and the Eastern sea-board of the United States). Endless accumulation and global climate change were not serious threats. Now the laws and social relations of capital (commodification and monetization) dominate pretty much everywhere. Endless accumulation and global climate change are serious dangers. But it is, Marx said as early as *The Communist Manifesto* of 1848, in the nature of capital to create the world market, to annihilate space through time, to enter into a spiral of endless accumulation, to revolutionize productive forces, and so on. Capital, unchallenged, inevitably expands geographically and intensifies its hold over us both here and ultimately everywhere. This is not primarily a moral issue but a scientific finding that has moral implications, as becomes abundantly clear from the moral outrage that suffuses the text of the first volume of *Capital*. In our own times, for example, endless accumulation produces environmental degradation which produces the moral outrage of the environmentalists.

Marx recognises, however, the contradictory character of the alienation that capital entails. Capital is not only destructive but a constructive and creative force that transforms the world in positive as well as in negative ways. In the *Grundrisse* (1973, pp. 409, 410) Marx acknowledges, without irony,

> the great civilizing influence of capital; its production of a stage of society in comparison to which all earlier ones appear as mere *local developments* of humanity and as *nature idolatry* … capital drives beyond national barriers and prejudices, as much as beyond nature worship, as well as all traditional, confined, complacent, encrusted satisfactions of present needs, and reproductions of old ways of life. It is destructive of all of this, and constantly revolutionizes it, tearing down all the barriers which hem in the development of the forces of production, the expansion of needs, the all-sided development of production, and the exploitation and exchange of natural and mental forces.

In passages of this sort Marx accepts individual and in some instances collective alienations as necessary to achieve a higher order social system in which improved material conditions can realise the promise of an unalienated life. Marx is not alone in arguing that sacrifices and losses (alienations) of this sort may be necessary to achieve a greater good. Adam Smith, for example, sought to reconcile the conflict between his moral sentiments and the cold calculus of competitive exchange by purporting to show how liberating the hidden hand of the market from state controls can produce a far greater state of material well-being in which everyone might equally share. This still remains the unfulfilled promise of liberalism. Polanyi (1957, pp. 256–258) likewise sees the sacrifice of individual freedoms as essential to the design of collective freedoms (e.g. of a welfare state) that would redound to the benefit of all. Debates of this sort are still with us. Republicans objected to the health care mandate in Obama's Affordable Care Act because it violated sacrosanct individual freedoms. The counter-argument is that all individuals will be better off in a society where everyone has instant access to adequate health care.

How individuals and social movements confront such contradictions becomes the big question. The individual psychologised (existential) alienation as articulated in Marx's early manuscripts here connects with a critique of the objective alienations produced through the reproduction of capital on the world market. Workers may accept the alienations of wage labour in return for sufficient access to commodities to fulfill their personal wants, needs and desires (Gorz, 1989). Alienated wage labour may be offset by compensatory consumerism. In the *Grundrisse* and *Capital* Marx notes how endless capital accumulation rests on the endless production and reproduction of wants, needs and desires backed by ability to pay. In the *The Economic and Philosophic Manuscripts,* Marx (1964, pp. 147, 148) notes how

> the extension of products and needs falls into contriving and ever-calculating *subservience* to inhuman, unnatural and imaginary appetites … This estrangement … produces sophistication of needs on the one hand and a bestial barbarization, a complete, unrefined, abstract simplicity of need, on the other.

Such contradictions operate through and across scales (from macro to micro and back again). Alienations felt and experienced by individuals in particular places and times exist in the context of alienations produced by capitalist processes of globalisation, time-space compression, accumulation by dispossession, land seizures, and the wholesale exploitation of billions of workers, men and women drawn from different cultural and geographical settings all around the world (Harvey, 2003, chap. 4).

Alienation exists almost everywhere. It exists in the labour process. The problem is not only that good-paying jobs are scarce but few jobs are meaningful and fulfilling.

Deindustrialization eliminated many jobs that were exploitative but meaningful (the steel worker in a bustling factory). Now we see the rise of jobs that are exploitative and meaningless (like TSA agent). Alienation from politics (e.g. traditional political parties) is everywhere. Resentments of a state apparatus that fails to reassure or facilitate greater freedoms are on the rise. Repressive regulatory regimes are producing oppositional movements embracing libertarianism. A climate of widespread non-ideological cultural anarchism takes hold. Regulatory impositions have increased exponentially everywhere. Daily life becomes increasingly frustrating and nightmarish: in the United States, fighting extra charges on telephone bills and credit cards and arguing over health insurance reimbursements consume more and more time. Bureaucratised corporations are every bit as bad as the state in relation to consumers. Their strategy is to deflect and discourage complaints rather than to deal with them. We all end up with less and less time for ourselves while household time-saving innovations are increasingly in evidence. Where is the promised transcendence?

The politics of alienation

Ken Loach's film, 'I, Daniel Blake' relates the trauma of an elderly person's encounter with the welfare services in Britain. These services, it becomes clear, are not designed to help people in need but to punish people for being needy. The good citizen is not needy. The film evokes obvious parallels in other sectors of social provision. Are the police there to help or to disciplines, surveil and repress us? Alienation dominates much of politics and daily life (Lefebvre, 1981).

So where are all the protest movements? In London the police kill an unarmed black man: a riot ensues and stores are looted and burned. Similar events occur in Stockholm and Paris. In Gezi Park in Istanbul an arbitrary decision to transform a central park into a shopping mall leads people to erupt in anger. They are met with police violence and repression, which sparks eve more anger. Within a few days the protest spreads throughout the whole urban system in Turkey. The lack of democracy becomes the problem. Such struggles are not labour struggles of the classic sort (Keller, 2013). They are outbreaks of popular discontent, of all those who are alienated in daily life no matter whether it's in the living space, the workspace, or wherever. Shortly after Gezi Park in the summer of 2013 a street action against rising transport fares spread like wildfire from city to city and to issue after issue in Brazil. Millions take to the streets in mass protests, only to meet with violent police repression.

The most typical response of alienated populations is to remain passive, resentful, morose and depressed (succumbing to drugs and alcohol) but to occasionally erupt in anger, frustration and rage, as happened in the London riots. At such moments people feel compelled to act. The system is rotten. They want to destroy the existing order of things. This was the case for many segments of the population around the USA in the summer of 2016. The anger had been steadily mounting after the broadly progressive global protests in Seattle in 1999 passing through the short but surprisingly influential Occupy movement of 2011 (which also spread within the United States as well as internationally). This last case was the movement that focused on Wall Street and the 'One Percent' as being at the center of contemporary ills, only to be greeted (almost in an act of unconscious affirmation of the importance of the political point) by fierce police repression mobilised at the behest of 'the Party of Wall Street'. To divert attention from capitalism's abject failures, the capitalist class fed the population racial minorities, women, and immigrants as easy targets for blame. The relentless scapegoating of immigrants, racial minorities and women proceeded a-pace.

This was the world in which right-wing populism and bigoted nationalist and racist movements began to thrive. With mass alienation, somebody like Trump could more easily come along and blast his way into power. Trump is the President of alienation, produced by alienation.

The production of alienation

But where does this alienation come from and why does it seem to be intensifying and proliferating? To begin with, transformations in the organisation of production and manufacturing – deindustrialization – over the last forty years have played a critical role. Meaningful jobs and the more or less solidarious communities that arose to support them (in cities like Detroit and Sheffield) have been disappearing in droves. A car plant in East Oxford and its working class community (Blackbird Leys) employed more than 20,000 workers in the 1960s but is reduced to 2000 by the mid 1990s. Deprived of the opportunity of making cars, alienated youth in Blackbird Leys took to joy-riding cars and participating in street riots against the police in 1991–1992 (Harvey & Hayter, 1993). Interestingly the shift of objective experience from the factory to the street was accompanied by an ideological shift from socialist to cultural anarchist aspirations. Anarchist elements were prominent in the Brazilian uprisings of 2013 as well as in the Occupy movement of 2011. Changing objective conditions produce shifts in political subjectivities.

The increasing industrialisation and capitalisation of agriculture has likewise destroyed the economic basis for a distinctive agrarian way of life. The rice farmers of South Korea commit suicide, peasant ways of life and culture disappear and, just as important, the small rural towns that once profitably serviced agrarian activities decline precipitously. Much of Trump's support and much of the Brexit vote in Britain came from small town and rural areas that were facing catastrophic economic decline, leaving no option for the young except to migrate to already overcrowded and high rent metropolitan areas in the hope of work. Germany is experiencing a similar collapse of traditional small town and village life providing fuel for a political movement of the far right.

New transport and communications systems have also helped dramatically change the landscapes of production and consumption. It is possible now for sophisticated engineering, design, innovation, and even marketing of a product to be located in the United States, while production occurs elsewhere. An assembly line can be across the Mexican border in Ciudad Juarez while research, design and administration can be in Dallas or Atlanta. The skills that exist in the United States can be combined seamlessly with cheap Mexican labour. The effect is to disempower labour in the USA. The argument that Trump makes about the consequences of NAFTA for workers is to some degree correct. NAFTA is not unique. German corporations do the same with Poland, for example. Such regional configurations are now emerging all over the place (Baldwin, 2016). The benefits mainly flow to corporate elites and their hangers-on while traditional working classes in the advanced capitalist countries are diminished both economically and politically. The social cohesion that once existed around factory labour gets torn to shreds.

Such trends intensify through the application of information technologies and artificial intelligence. A production line in Mexico can be controlled from an office in Dallas. It will also soon be possible to organise driverless delivery trucks and pilotless planes. There is an on-going but accelerating reconfiguration of the global workforce and its employment prospects. Two thirds of the job losses over the last forty years are thought to be from technological change. But in addition, work forces in the USA, Europe of Japan now have to compete with the workforces elsewhere. In the 1960s labourers in the advanced capitalist countries were protected against foreign competition and could organise to procure better wages and better living conditions within the boundaries of their state. But that privilege eroded through neoliberal globalisation and the increasing competition between labour forces around the world. And that of course means that in many places jobs do disappear never to return (McKinsey Global Institute, 2012). The argument that many jobs go to Mexico or China is partly correct. The fear that they might go is a powerful tool to drive wages down.

The geography of it all

What we are seeing is the creation of regional configurations of production and exchange under the control of some dominant class and corporate power. Capitalists create privileged regional spaces of economic activity from which they can exclusively benefit, while the working populations in their backyards gain little or nothing. The working people of the U.S don't benefit from NAFTA any more than the working people of Germany benefit from the European Union. Within each regional power block there is a hegemonic power. German capital has been the primary beneficiary of the construction of the Euro-Zone, while Greece has had value sucked dry by German and French finance capital. The U.S tried to set up something similar (the TPP) to do the same in the Pacific. When Trump abandoned the project (even though it would have been of great interest to the US ruling classes) China stepped in. Regional reorganizations are occurring everywhere. The effect is to reconfigure how the world's labour force is mobilised for the benefit of capitalist classes and technological elites the world around.

The rate of change is accelerating. Once upon a time the textile mills were in Lowell, Massachusetts and then they went to the Carolinas and then they went to Mexico and then to Bangladesh. It took about 30, 40, 50 years for all of that to happen so adaptation initially could be slow. But what we are now seeing is a speed-up that is hard to adapt to. This speed-up largely derives from the second potentially fatal contradiction of exponential growth. The cotton mills in Baltimore were at their height in 1920s and did not finally disappear until 1970. But now, recalcitrant populations suddenly find themselves bereft; advantages they thought they had disappear overnight. Furthermore, the world's wage labour force has expanded dramatically. Since 1980 it has gone from around 2–3 billion (McKinsey Global Institute, 2012). Most of China's population has come in, all of Indonesia, large segments of India, so we now have manufacturing going on in all these countries and rapid offshoring of manufacturing even from China to Bangladesh, Vietnam, Cambodia and the like.

There is something unusual about this, however. Industrialisation no longer guarantees a move very far up the GDP per capita table (as used to be the case before 1970 or so). It guarantees increasing inequality instead.

There is a very simple reason for this. A US-based corporation like Apple Computer has a high rate of profit, around 28%. FoxConn, which makes the computers in Shenzhen has a profit rate around 3%, employing a huge labour force (now about to be made redundant

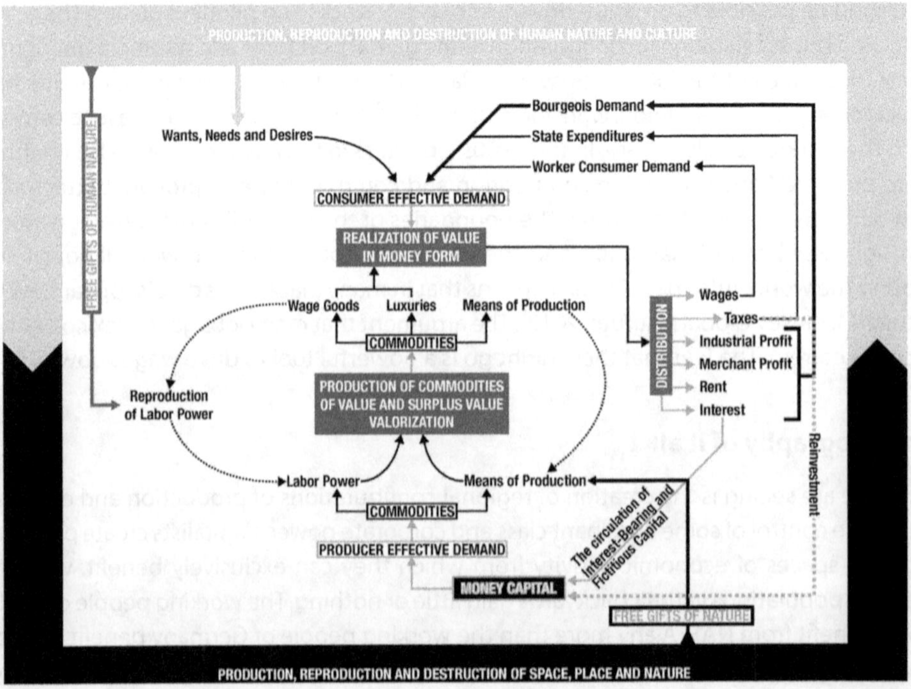

Figure 1. The Circulation of Capital According to Marx.

by automation). There is an increasing gap between where value is created and where it is realised. Walmart, the Gap, Ikea, and the like, make their money out of value produced elsewhere. Conditions in the overall labour force are undergoing a radical reconfiguration. The biggest employers of labour in the USA in the 1960s were General Motors, Ford, and US Steel. Now it is the holding companies of McDonalds, Kentucky Fried Chicken and WalMart. In these latter fields, the labour supply is largely precarious. The culture of young people in relationship to job opportunities is being revolutionized. They work in a coffee bar for six months and then go somewhere else. From a traditional perspective, this looks a terrible situation, but many younger people seem to like it. Even the college educated are getting used to a precarious peripatetic lifestyle that matches the evolving structure of job opportunities. This appears to them as a peculiar kind of freedom compared to a structure of labour opportunities that attaches one person to a particular niche in the division of labour for life. It is the perverse realisation of that brief glimpse of a different world that Marx sees in the first volume of *Capital* (617–618).

> Large scale industry, by its very nature, necessitates variation of labour, fluidity of functions, and mobility of the worker in all directions ... The partially developed individual, who is the bearer of one specialized social function, must be replaced by the totally developed individual, for whom the different social functions are different modes of activity he takes up in turn.

The circulation of capital and the production of alienation

How can we put all of this together to get a picture of how capital in general works? Consider the circulation of capital as a whole, as a totality (see Figure 1; Harvey, 2017). There are three key moments in the circulation process. One is the moment of production where capital is, as Marx put it, 'valorized' by labourers producing commodities. The moment of realisation follows, where the value created in commodity form is monetized through a sale in the market. Then there is the moment of distribution when the realised money is allocated between labour, various factions of capital (landlords, merchants, financiers as well as industrial producers) and the state. Capital circulates through all these moments.

This perspective of the totality of circulation is vital to reconstructing Marx's laws of motion of capital and the alienations that attach thereto. It is a fantasy, for example, to think that financialization is a recent feature to capital accumulation. Marx shows in Volume 3 of *Capital* that the separation of interest-bearing capital as a property relation from the circuit of industrial capital produces distinctive contradictions. The crises of 1847–1848 and 1857 are analysed as commercial and monetary crises. There is an uncanny resemblance between Marx's descriptions of these crises and what happened in 2007–2008 in the United States (see Harvey, 2017, p. 202). The losses were widespread and decisive. Marx even notes how the defective institutionalisation of the Bank of England in 1844 played a role in deepening and extending those crises (much as the European Central Bank played a negative role from 2010 onwards in Europe)The separation of ownership from management likewise produced critical tensions in the management of accumulation. Only in these terms can we make sense of Giovanni Arrighi's detailed historical reconstruction of how hegemonic shifts in capitalist power relations on the world stage (such as the shift from the Low Countries to Britain in the eighteenth century) are preceded by and to some degree accomplished through a strong phase of financialization.

What is the driving force that keeps capital circulating? The classic answer is the search for profit on the part of capitalists and capitalist corporations. The focus is then on the moment of production. Profit comes, Marx shows, from alienating labour and extracting surplus labour and surplus value. The exploitation of living labour in production is the origin of profit. But the capitalist has also to realise and monetize the value congealed in the commodity through a sale in the market. This presumes there is a want need and demand for the commodity backed by sufficient money for potential consumers to be able to pay.

What happens if there is no sale either because there is no want, need or desire or because of an inability to pay? This sometimes happens and in the 1930s it was massively so. There is no possibility of profit. Capitalists and corporations stop investing or employing labour. The economy goes into a downward spiral. It then becomes critical to create a demand so that capital can realise a profit. The Keynesian solution is to do this by ratcheting up state expenditures (for this, military budgets are a perfect instantaneous tool provided an adequate enemy threat is first manufactured). The strategy of aggregate demand management, largely organised through the state, focusses on the moment of realisation. This becomes a second driver of accumulation through circulation. A lot of contemporary economic struggles now occur at the point of realisation rather than at the point of production. But such struggles have a different structure and logic from those that occur at the point of production. Workers act as buyers not as workers when they are in the market place (Marx, 1973, pp. 419–422). Conflicts at the point of realisation are between buyers and sellers. This is very different from struggles that pit capital against labour. This is what Marx refers to as 'profit upon alienation' (profit taken at the point of commodity trading).

If there is a struggle against rising rents or scamming on broad band services, for example, then all kinds of social groups will likely become involved. It is not just workers, but middle class and petty bourgeois factions (shopkeepers and restaurant owners as well as professionals) who are affected. The way property prices and rents are surging in New York City is at the center of broad-based discontent. A movement against the rising rents and speculation in property markets would draw support from many different groups within the population. The protestors on the streets of Brazilian cities in June of 2013 or those who took part in Gezi Park protest in Istanbul, were not from the classic working class (though many workers did ultimately join in). They were made up of a complex mix of people including disaffected and alienated middle class groups in the population with a variety of demands and interests. In Brazil the issues were increasing transport costs, investments in spectacular events like the World Cup and the Olympics at the expense of social expenditures on health care, education and housing, to say nothing of rampant corruption. Rising food prices have long been one of the main triggers of the uprisings in North Africa and the Middle East (Walton & Seddon, 1994).

In addition there are all those who have long been seeking to create heterotopic spaces where they could live a relatively unalienated existence. Such movements exist all over the place. They can be found in the heart of metropolitan centers as well as on the rural margins. Many of the major protests since 2000 or so have been animated by groups of this sort. Urban movements of discontent are on the rise in particular. They are often movements of populations alienated by the deteriorating conditions of daily life in the city and the lack of any kind of democracy (Lefebvre, 1981). They demand empowerment and ways to ameliorate their increasing marginalisation as citizens rather than as workers. These sorts of struggle are qualitatively different to the traditional labour struggles around factory work. As factories disappear in many parts of the world, one cutting edge of anti-capitalist struggles lies in the field of realisation rather than production.

But where do the state expenditures laid out for purposes of demand management come from? If the economy is in a downward spiral then tax receipts will fall. Raising taxes will diminish not augment consumer demand. The state has therefore to create money; it has to borrow and deficit finance to push the economy into an upward spiral. But where can it borrow from? It turns out that there are mediating organizations within the circulation process – banks and financial institutions – that command surplus money power and have the power to leverage surpluses in effect creating ever more money. This is another source of the energy that propels the capitalist accumulation system onwards and upwards. Those who have surplus funds want to put their money to work to earn a dividend. I have a private pension fund. TIAA has a fiduciary responsibility to me to put my pension money to work and get the highest rate of return. TIAA offers credit. It incentivizes people to borrow money and to engage in profit-seeking. My pension fund stands accused of funding land grabs in Latin America.

Debt and alienation

Debt is a claim on future labour. The money value of my pension in five years' time depends upon value production over the next five years. Pension funds are just one example out of many institutions that engage with debt creation. There are the stock and bond holders. Banks store other people's money and use it to make profit for themselves. All these institutions want a rate of return. For this reason they push the system of endless accumulation as hard as they can. In times of overaccumulation and surplus liquidity, institutions literally knock on people's doors begging them to borrow.

Right now, the prime source of energy behind the circulation of capital lies with financial institutions in the field of distribution. They create the debt and issue the credit which should then be redeemed through valorization. If valorization flags, then one way out is to borrow even more (politely called 'rolling over the debt'). In this case, a Ponzi short-circuiting scheme is created. There is a good deal of evidence suggesting this is so.

If debt is a claim upon future labour then the future is foreclosed by taking on debt. This has a positive outcome if the borrowed money is valorized through production. But it quickly turns negative if the debts cannot be valorized. Debt is a key form of social control for capital and, as such, a key dource of alienation. Our future is dictated by the need to redeem our past debts. The result is a society based on debt peonage (Hudson, 2015). Capitalists understand this very well. When, for example, mortgage finance was set up in the 1930s to encourage working class homeownership as a sign of fulfillment of the American Dream, it was noted that 'debt-encumbered homeowners don't go on strike'. Likewise, debt-encumbered students don't cause trouble. The whole debt structure forms a vast network of social control that curtails basic freedoms and exaggerates those feelings of alienation with which I began.

Such alienations pervade contemporary politics. When Bill Clinton won the Presidency in 1992, he outlined his ambitions for a new economic program. His Treasury Secretary, Robert Rubin (from Goldman Sachs) objected. When Clinton asked 'Why?' Rubin said 'Wall Street bond holders won't let you'. Clinton's famous response was: 'You mean to say that my whole economic program is held hostage to a bunch of fucking bond traders on Wall Street?' Clinton came to the Presidency promising universal healthcare and delivered NAFTA, the reform of welfare as we know it, a vicious reform of the criminal justice system that led to the mass incarceration of mainly racial minorities, a reform of housing finance that culminated in the foreclosure disaster of 2007–2008, and the repeal of the Glass-Steagall regulatory frameworks that constrained speculative activity on the part of banks. And that is what the bond holders wanted. This poses a big question: who is really in charge, the politicians or the bondholders? The answer is clear in the case of Greece: it is the bondholders. The 2017 tax reform in the United States is a bond-holder's charter that delivers immense benefits to the oligarchs while in the long-run dispossessing the people and accelerating debt creation. It opens the path to a competition over accumulation by dispossession on the world-stage. The next step in the USA is to cut essential social programs, such as Social Security, Medicare and Medicaid, which are crucial economic supports for the mass of the population, in order to redeem the debt that has been used to fill the coffers of the oligarchs.

Under such conditions democracy becomes a sham. Everyone knows that most political parties and national governments are under the control of the bondholders and that the equivalent of the Party of Wall Street is what really rules (the Treasury Secretary of the US government has come from Goldman Sachs for most of the time during successive presidencies since 1993). As a result, alienation from politics and distrust of political parties become a norm, as does an acceleration in the growth of debt peonage.

Credit, endless growth and the production of alienation

Credit money is, it turns out, the only form of capital that can increase without limit. Us values can, of course, increase dramatically. China in two years consumed 45% more cement than the United States had consumed in 100 years before that. China in 2007 had zero miles of high-speed train network. It now has fifteen thousand miles. What has happened in China in terms of productive activity and the creation of new us value is astonishing. In 2008, the Chinese had to find a way to employ 20 million people who had lost their jobs because of the crash in the US consumer market. By early 2009 they apparently had a net job loss, according to the IMF/ILO (2010) report, of 3 million. They created 17 million jobs in about 9 months by investment in massive physical infrastructures and whole new cities. They consumed more than half of the world's cement, more than half of the world's steel, about 60% of the world's copper. During this whole period commodity prices rose. Those countries producing raw materials for China, such as Chile, Brazil and Australia, quickly came out of the 2007–2008 collapse. But the prospect of endless exponential growth in the use of cement is terrifying. China is experiencing chronic environmental problems as a result. The Chinese also went from a low to high debt to GDP ratio in a very few years. They became leading participants in the debt-creation game. Fortunately they are mainly indebted in their own currency so they can avoid the fate of Greece or other heavily indebted countries that were forced by their creditors to implement savage austerity programs to pay off their creditors. But the Chinese debt is now viewed as a serious problem: how might it be redeemed?

This is a key global problem. The IMF reports global debt has been growing exponentially since the 1970s (International Monetary Fund, 2016). There was a little blip in 2008 when it went down a bit but it jumped up again shortly thereafter. This is Ponzi finance and escalating debt peonage in action on a global scale. The experts in the management and manipulation of debt peonage (the hedge funds, the private equity investors and the investment banks) come out on top. They are managing the global economy in their own interest. Trump appoints experts from Goldman Sachs to manage the economy. They typically earned their billions not by making anything but by legally robbing people of their asset values. Trump's Treasury Secretary Mnuchin took over a failing bank heavily invested in real estate and turned it around by forcing evictions and replacing affordable housing by upscale residential accommodations. This is not a labour problem. Manipulators of this sort made out like bandits from the housing foreclosures and evictions that occurred in 2007–2008. George Soros legally robbed the British people of more than a billion dollars over seven days by betting against the valuation of the British pound against the German deutschmark in 1992. Then everyone is surprised at the incredible increase in wealth inequalities in the capitalist world. What impact does all this have on the alienation of populations?

This gets me back to the roots of the deep discontent with this system. At some point there will be a revolt against debt peonage. I am surprised that the student debt movement didn't morph into a massive oppositional movement. A moratorium on debt or a jubilee could wipe out all debt. But that would include my pension fund. This cannot occur without guaranteeing future pension incomes by other means. It is difficult to create mass solidarity among many individual debtors some of whom have already paid off a significant part of their debt and would resent a younger generation escaping such a burden. State nationalisation of private pension funds would be the only answer.

Bond holder power and the state-finance nexus

At this point we are all locked in. We have to support the system because if we do not then we are the ones who get screwed. We are all locked into a system of debt peonage. This seems a perfect recipe for the production of mass alienation. The state, as it is currently structured, cannot deal with it, because, as Bill Clinton was so clearly told, governments are dependent entirely on the power of the bondholders. If they go against that power, the state loses its financial base. At the center of it all lies what I call the state finance nexus, – the unseemly and often unstable alliance between central banks (the pinnacle of the private financial system) and the treasury departments (the arbiter of power within the state). This is the nexus of power that locks all of us into debt peonage and a foreclosed future. The big, big question is how do we escape the clutches of the state-finance nexus? What forms of social movement can help us get out? There are lots of heterotopic spaces emerging where people try and live an alternative life and contract out of the debt economy. They are searching for some other way to live and refuse to get locked in. The belated hope is that somewhere and somehow a parallel form of governing and financing (perhaps with local currencies) will allow more and more people to escape into a world of unalienated social relations and autonomous forms of production and consumption. Such an anarchist strategy is unlikely to succeed. The power of the state-finance nexus has to be confronted directly. The history of the Greek problem illustrates how hard that will be.

But we also have to understand that we are also a key part of the problem. It not just the dominant capitalist class and their hangers on who are actively engaged in foreclosing our future in order to ensure the perpetual growth of their monetary power. We are all caught in a trap. The unassuming peasant who falls for the trap of microfinance and the pensioner who demands assurances of their own financial future are all caught up in this system of debt peonage. Until we understand that and act consciously to get ourselves out of this trap, then we are not going to be able to do anything other than keep on going with the global Ponzi scheme, where debt and money will be created without limit for the benefit of a financialized capitalist class. Privileged classes will use the circulation process in such a way as to extract as much personal wealth and power as they can and while the opportunity lasts. Since 2007–2008 almost all of the gains from the recovery have gone into the pockets of the top 1%. They are by and large doing just fine. For the rest of us, the objective alienation of whatever wealth we have by the ruling classes leaves behind a bitter residue of subjective alienation from the kind of political economy that capital has constructed.

We have, in short, an amazing situation where the capitalist classes are everywhere doing extremely well, while capital in general is doing rather badly. The capitalist class will do nothing about such a situation. They have no incentive to change. And many of us are also in a situation where we do not have an immediate incentive to do anything about it either – I totally lose my pension, my house and property as financial assets if the state-finance nexus, the Bastille of contemporary capitalism, is stormed by angry mobs. This is the political dilemma inherent in the current situation. While our task may be to change the world, it is a prerequisite for revolutionary theory that we first understand it. The theory of objective alienation along with an understanding of its subjective consequences is one vital key to unlock the door of a progressive politics for the future.

Disclosure statement

No potential conflict of interest was reported by the author.

References

Baldwin, R. (2016). *The great convergence: Information, technology and the new globalization*. Cambridge, MA: Belknap Press.

Gorz, A. (1989). *Critique of economic reason*. London: Verso.

Harvey, D. (2003). *The new imperialism*. Oxford: Oxford University Press.

Harvey, D. (2014). *Seventeen contradictions and the end of capitalism*. London / New York, NY: Profile Press / Oxford University Press.

Harvey, D. (2017). *Marx, capital and the madness of economic reason*. London / New York, NY: Profile Press / Oxford University Press.

Harvey, D., & Hayter, T. (1993). *The factory in the city: The story of the Cowley automobile workers in Oxford*. Brighton: Mansell.

Hudson, M. (2015). *Killing the host: How financial parasites and debt destroy the global economy*. ISLET-Verlag.

International Monetary Fund/International Labour Organisation. (2010). The challenges of growth, employment and social cohesion. Discussion paper, Joint ILO-IMF Conference in Cooperation with the Prime Minister of Norway. Retrieved from http://www.osloconference2010.org/discussionpaper.pdf

International Monetary Fund. (2016, October). Debt: Use it wisely. *Fiscal Monitor: World Economic and Financial Surveys*. Washington, D.C.

Jaeggi, R. (2014). *Alienation*. New York, NY: Columbia University Press.

Keller, B. (2013, June 30). The revolt of the rising classes. *The New York Times*.

Lefebvre, H. (1981). *The critique of everyday life*. London: Verso.

Marx, K. (1964). *The economic and philosophic manuscripts of 1844*. New York, NY: International Publishers.

Marx, K. (1973). *Grundrisse*. London: Penguin.

McKinsey Global Institute. (2012). *The world at work: Jobs, pay and skills for 3.5 billion people*. New York: Report of the McKinsey Global Institute.

Mesjaros, I. (1970). *Marx's theory of alienation*. London: Merlin Press.

Ollman, B. (1972). *Alienation: Marx's conception of man in capitalist society*. Cambridge: Cambridge University Press.

Polanyi, K. (1957). *The great transformation: The political and economic origins of our time*. Boston, MA: Beacon Press.

Walton, J., & Seddon, D. (1994). *Free markets and food riots: The politics of global adjustment*. New York, NY: Wiley.

Zhang, Y. (2011). *The subjective dimension of Marxist historical dialectics*. Berlin: CANut International Publishers.

Zhang, Y. (2014). *Back to Marx: Changes of philosophical discourse in the context of economics*. Gottingen: Universitatsverlag Gottingen.

6 The enduring regulation of the poor

Frances Fox Piven

Some 41 million Americans, many of them children, currently live below the official poverty level. As a proportion of the population, the number has been stable for several decades. But what it means to be officially poor has changed. Since the calculation of the poverty level is based largely on the cost of food, and food costs have risen much more slowly than other basic costs, the Congressional Research Service estimates that the numbers who cannot afford basic necessities are actually three times higher than the official poverty rate.

At first blush, these facts can be seen as something of a puzzle, if only because the United States is enormously wealthy and, considered simply as a policy design problem, the solutions would seem to be near at hand. We could, for example, as the women in the 1960s welfare rights movement used to demand, simply give the poor money, a guaranteed income of some sort, and the funds could be recouped by closing a few of the tax loopholes for the wealthy that have widened steadily in the past few decades. Or as some liberals tirelessly argue, we could cut expenditures on armaments and military bases. Or, instead of taking the large policy step of creating a guaranteed income, we could simply fund the programs that now provide nutritional or housing or health care or childcare benefits more generously, and administer them more generously as well, as most other rich countries do. Needless to say, such policy changes are exceedingly unlikely in the current political environment. Indeed such programs as we do fund are regularly targeted for polemical attack and budget cuts by Republican majorities in the Congress and in the state legislatures.

Why, then, the failure to reduce or eliminate poverty? Well, of course the numerous rent-seeking interest groups entwined with government oppose liberalizing initiatives and instead press for more and more tax cuts, and more and more expenditures from which they can reap a handsome profit, all the while complaining about the failure of the poor to somehow pull themselves out of poverty by their own efforts. The budget currently before the congress includes hundreds of billions in cuts to programs that benefit the worst-off, in anticipation of tax 'reforms' that benefit the best-off. This is surely part of the reason. But there is no outrage from democratic publics at our neglect either. Indeed, most of the time, there isn't even outrage from the poor themselves.

I think the dynamics that result in our harsh treatment of the poor are deeper and more pervasive than the distortions of democratic will that result from the machinations of interest group politics, and that ultimately these deeper dynamics explain not only our poverty policies (which after all directly affect only a minority of the population), but our helplessness in the face of spiraling inequality that affects all of us. The problem is not simply economic, it is also cultural and the cultural and economic practices that sustain high levels of poverty are embedded in our policy institutions.

A very long time ago, Richard Cloward and I began to study the American system of poor relief known of course as 'welfare.' Our interest was provoked by our work at a project on the Lower East Side of New York City called Mobilization for Youth, a forerunner of the national 'war on poverty' of the 1960s. Our experience there first exposed us to street level welfare practices, and then led us to work with grass roots groups of poor mothers trying to improve those practices. These groups eventually joined together in the 'welfare rights' movement of the 1960s.

What we learned about abusive and lawless welfare practices was, we thought, astonishing, but it was not easy to get enlightenment about the causes of these practices. Our colleagues, mainly social policy experts at the Columbia University School of Social Work, had little interest in our reports, seeming to doubt their veracity. We turned instead to historical work on poor relief in the U.S. and especially to the rich historical work on poverty and poor relief in England. In 1971 we published our conclusions in a book called *Regulating the Poor: the Functions of Public Welfare.* The functions that we thought explained our mean-spirited assistance to the poor reflected a longstanding historical pattern. When shifts or downturns in markets led to widespread hardship with ensuing unruliness and protest, elites were likely to initiate some kind of assistance or relief. Even then, and even when work was not available, assistance was always conditioned by the terms of what the English poor law commissioners had called the principle of 'less eligibility,' meaning that no one on the dole should be as well off as even the meanest laborer. And once order was restored even that assistance was likely to be withdrawn, at least from the able-bodied. Those of the aged and infirm who were allowed to remain on the dole were treated as spectacles of misery and degradation, thus underlining to all who could see the work-enforcing message of the principle of less eligibility. While we no longer shame the pauper by branding and displaying her in the marketplace, we still publicly shame her, to teach the lesson that there is a worse fate than low wage work.

This interpretation created a small furor in social welfare circles whose spokespeople were inclined to emphasize the role of social welfare in our steady progress toward a more humane society. But ensuing events upturned these customary narratives.

Welfare and other policies directed to the poor had expanded as the black freedom movement exploded in the Northern cities. But the movement subsided in the 1970s, in part assuaged by concessionary policies, and also as a result of the absorption of movement leaders into normal politics. In 1968 Republicans gained the Presidency, deploying a rhetoric that took aim at 'welfare queens' for special insult. Then the cutbacks began in earnest, and welfare programs were a special target. Work requirements proliferated, benefit levels fell, the monitoring, and criminalization of recipients escalated, and legal assistance for the poor was slashed. The turn in policy was not really partisan. When Bill Clinton campaigned for the presidency in 1992 he coined the slogan 'end welfare as we know it.' He went far to fulfilling the promise when he signed the Personal Responsibility Act of 1996 which led to plummeting welfare rolls and sharply reduced benefits, policy shifts that meshed neatly the with stagnant and declining wages and harsher working conditions of the neoliberal era. In the decades since, the principle of less eligibility has reigned unchallenged.

But not everywhere. If we lift our eyes from the disheartening trends in the U.S. (and, albeit to a lesser extent, in other rich AND CAPITALIST countries in the West), a remarkable development is apparent, particularly in middle income countries in the global South. China, India, Brazil, Indonesia, Turkey, South Africa, Mexico and China have inaugurated social assistance programs that reach over a billion people with cash and 'in-kind' benefits that often provide a large share of the income of recipients, and in some countries have made a large dent in the population in poverty. These new programs are often called 'conditional cash assistance' but in fact they tend to minimize the conditions for assistance, thus breaking sharply with the poor relief tradition. It is noteworthy also that these are countries where the numerous and often unruly poor have played a large role in both local and national politics. As earlier in the West, it is the politics of the poor, often obscured by our failure to recognize the riot, the rebellion and other behaviors we call criminal or deviant as politics at all, that compels the initiation of humanizing and equalizing income assistance.

Disclosure statement

No potential conflict of interest was reported by the author.

7 Governmentality, subjectivity, and the neoliberal form of life

Daniele Lorenzini

ABSTRACT
In this paper, I argue that the appropriate answer to the question of the form contemporary neoliberalism gives our lives rests on Michel Foucault's definition of neoliberalism as a particular art of governing human beings. I claim that Foucault's definition consists in three components: neoliberalism as a set of technologies structuring the 'milieu' of individuals in order to obtain specific effects from their behavior; neoliberalism as a governmental rationality transforming individual freedom into the very instrument through which individuals are directed; and neoliberalism as a set of political strategies that constitute a specific, and eminently governable, form of subjectivity. I conclude by emphasising the importance that Foucault's work on neoliberalism as well as the ancient 'ethics of the care of the self' still holds for us today.

Introduction

What form does contemporary neoliberalism give our lives? I address this question through a critical discussion of Michel Foucault's work on neoliberalism and the growing (polemical) literature on this theme. On the one hand, defenders of neoliberalism usually define it as a set of political and economic strategies that give individuals an unprecedented opportunity to exercise their freedom far and wide, without imposing any specific form of life on them. On the other, many scholars, particularly those who adopt materialist positions, argue that, far from being emancipatory, neoliberalism is inherently oppressive because it perpetuates and radicalises the economic and social domination of the few over the many. In this paper, I will show that Foucault's analyses allow us to recognise that this very dichotomy – emancipation vs. oppression – fails to account for the singularity and complexity of the specific form of governmentality termed 'neoliberalism,' and that his notion of an 'ethics of the care of the self,' far from being modeled on the neoliberal subject, still possesses a critical significance for us today.

First of all, how exactly are we to define neoliberalism? In *The new way of the world*, Pierre Dardot and Christian Laval argue that traditional Marxist approaches are incapable of accounting for neoliberalism in its distinctiveness, since they tend to reduce it to the logic either of capitalism or of capital accumulation (Dardot & Laval, 2013). Foucault makes a similar point almost thirty years prior. In his lectures at the Collège de France on *The birth of biopolitics*, he questions three misleading ideas: first, that 'from the economic point of view neoliberalism is no more than the reactivation of old, secondhand economic theories'; second, that 'from the sociological point of view it is just a way of establishing strictly market relations in society'; and third, that 'from a political point of view [it] is no more than a cover for a generalised administrative intervention by the state' (Foucault, 2008, p. 130). These three wrong-headed characterisations, Foucault argues, ultimately make neoliberalism out to be 'nothing at all,' thus failing to grasp its uniqueness (p. 130). Indeed, neoliberalism cannot and should not simply be reduced to classical liberalism or to market society. What, then, does Foucault take neoliberalism to be?

Foucault's answer is that neoliberalism is first and foremost a specific *rationality* or *art of government*. Seen from this point of view, it simultaneously constitutes both a prolongation and a rupture vis-à-vis classical liberalism, or better, it pushes classical liberalism to its limits. In fact, according to Foucault, if the problem for Adam Smith was 'how to cut out or contrive a free space of the market within an already given political society,' neoliberalism raises a different issue, which is nevertheless a 'radicalization' of this classical one and which consists in asking 'how the overall exercise of political power can be modeled on the principles of a market economy' (p. 131). Therefore, neoliberalism is not only *laissez-faire*, but also, and more significantly, a specific way of organising social relations on the basis of a rationality dictated by the market; it is a complex set of governmental technologies whose aim is to shape individual and collective conduct thus constituting 'subjects' in a completely novel fashion. This is why the question of the form neoliberalism gives our subjectivities and lives acquires a crucial political and ethical significance.[1]

In order to explore the main features of Foucault's definition of neoliberalism as a particular art of governing human beings, I will focus on three (deeply interconnected) points: the action or intervention on the environment (*'milieu'*), the question of individual freedom and 'critical ethos,' and the constitution of a specific form of subjectivity.

'Environmental' action and the issue of normativity

The first point to emphasise is that, according to Foucault, neoliberal governmentality consists primarily in an 'environmental' action, that is, in a set of mechanisms and technologies structuring the milieu of individuals in order to obtain specific effects from their behavior.[2] In *The birth of biopolitics*, Foucault insists on a crucial difference between classical liberalism and neoliberalism, referring in particular to Gary Becker's works. While in the eighteenth century *homo oeconomicus* 'basically functions as what could be called an intangible element with regard to the exercise of power' since, as 'the subject or object of *laissez-faire*,' she is conceived of as a person who must be left alone, for Becker, *homo oeconomicus* becomes a person 'who responds systematically to modifications in the variables of the environment' (p. 270). Therefore, she appears as someone 'manageable,' someone who 'responds systematically to systematic modifications artificially introduced into the environment' (p. 270). In other words, the neoliberal subject is 'someone who is eminently governable': she is no longer the 'intangible partner of *laissez-faire*,' but 'the correlate of a governmentality which will act on the environment and systematically modify its variables' (pp. 270, 271).

In this respect, the ordoliberalism of pre- and post-war Germany constitutes the transition point between classical liberalism and contemporary neoliberalism. Indeed, 'instead of accepting a free market defined by the state and kept … under state supervision,' ordoliberals claim that the free market should be the 'regulating principle of the state' (p. 116), and they conceive of the action on the milieu as a way of artificially organising a certain number of social and political conditions in order to allow competition to produce its effects (pp. 146, 147). Thus, German ordoliberals elaborate a social philosophy whose objective is not to intervene directly on market processes, but rather to give form to the 'environment' within which such processes function (Taylan, 2013, p. 82), that is, the 'social environment,' *die soziale Umwelt*, of the economic actors (Foucault, 2008, p. 146). While the interventionism initially advocated by Walter Eucken in the 1930s and 1940s was limited to the juridical framework of the market, the *Vitalpolitik* developed by Alexander Rüstow in the 1950s was instead a heavy socio-institutional interventionism aimed at producing its effects upon the 'worker's whole vital situation, his real, concrete situation, from morning to night and from night to morning,' in order to better integrate the worker's material and social life within the logic of the market (p. 157). Hence, Foucault argues that German ordoliberalism is an art of government that intervenes 'on society as such, in its fabric and depth' – that is, on the urban space, on education, on working conditions, etc. – 'so that competitive mechanisms can play a regulatory role at every moment and every point in society': it is not (only) an 'economic government,' but 'a government of society' as such (pp. 145, 146).

Although German ordoliberalism anticipates many aspects of contemporary neoliberalism, as inaugurated by the Chicago School, the kind of action on the milieu theorised by Chicago economists rests on different presuppositions. As I have already mentioned, Foucault refers to Becker's definition of economics as 'the science of the systematic nature of responses to environmental variables' (p. 269). This definition, according to Foucault, entails a profound transformation of the notion of *homo oeconomicus*, who goes from being the subject and object of *laissez-faire* to the subject and object of a particular form of governmentality. Indeed, while respecting the autonomy of market processes, the neoliberal art of government heavily intervenes on the social field in order to shape the conduct of individuals, inciting them to act in a specific way and modifying their environment so as to alter their behavior. However, Foucault makes clear that classical liberalism was itself already an art of government, since the subject of interest was never *really* left alone (pp. 275, 276). If the market economy could function exclusively through the pursuit of individual interests, it would not have been necessary to elaborate *neoliberal* technologies of government (Taylan, 2013, pp. 85, 86).

In recent years, scholars have argued that Foucault was so taken by neoliberalism that *The birth of biopolitics* serves as a defense of it (Behrent, 2009; de Lagasnerie, 2012; Zamora, 2014). François Ewald, in a seminar held at the University of Chicago with Gary Becker himself, claimed that Foucault saw Becker's work 'as creating the possibility to promote, to envision new kinds of liberty,' since Becker's theory of regulation 'makes it possible to conduct the behavior of the other without coercion, by incitation' (Ewald in Becker, Ewald, & Harcourt, 2012, p. 6). Therefore, according to Ewald, Becker's redefinition of *homo oeconomicus* is 'very close to what Foucault searched for with his theory of the subject and of subjectivity' in the last years of his life (p. 7). This interpretation of Foucault's position on neoliberalism continues to be widely invoked in order to praise or criticise Foucault's work in the 1980s on the ethics of the care of the self (Ball & Olmedo, 2013; Dilts, 2011; Nicoli & Paltrinieri, 2017). I will return to this issue at the close of this paper. I first want to discuss the claim that Foucault considered Becker's analyses as (potentially) promoting new kinds of freedom given that neoliberal governmentality conducts individual behavior by incitation and not by coercion.

While it might seem self-evident to point out that Ewald's interpretation of Foucault's position is not equivalent to Foucault's own framing of this discussion, several scholars have recently confused the two. For example, in their book *State phobia and civil society*, Mitchell Dean and Kaspar Villadsen fail to differentiate between Foucault's claims and Ewald's claims about Foucault. Following Michael Behrent (2010), they argue that we should study Ewald's intellectual and political trajectory if we want to understand Foucault's own thought, since Ewald is 'the most influential and loyal Foucauldian today' (Dean & Villadsen, 2016, p. 146). This line of argument is completely groundless, both from a historical and a philosophical point of view. Indeed, if we take seriously Foucault's *explicit* claim that (at least some) neoliberal governmental technologies exert a specific 'environmental' action in order to concretely, even if indirectly, shape individual conduct, it suddenly becomes hard to find convincing arguments to defend the picture of Foucault as an apologist of neoliberalism. The only way we can do so is if we attribute to him, as Dean and Villadsen do (p. 8), the normative claim according to which *this* specific modality of governing individuals (through an action on the milieu that 'incites' them to behave in certain ways) is better than *any* other form of power or governmentality directly 'coercing' them, and therefore that criticising neoliberalism would be a mistake, both theoretically and politically.

The problem with this claim is that Foucault never suggested anything of the sort in any of his works. Ben Golder has recently made this point very clear in responding to the well-known objections by Jürgen Habermas and Nancy Fraser according to which 'any attempt by Foucault at critique and resistance is necessarily disabled by the lack of normative grounds' (Golder, 2015, p. 17). Like it or not, in Foucault's work, critique and resistance have no normative grounds, since power and governmentality *in themselves* are not good or bad; they are just a fact of human life and human societies (Foucault, 1997, pp. 298, 299). This is why it is extremely difficult to claim that Foucault conceived of neoliberalism as giving more individual autonomy to a *homo oeconomicus* whose malleability it continuously produces and exploits (Taylan, 2013, pp. 77, 78). In other words, as I will show in the next section, what Dean and Villadsen seem to *deny* is the fact that, for Foucault, it is always possible, legitimate, and even necessary to raise the question of the 'acceptability' of neoliberal technologies of government, as well as any other mechanism of power – the question, that is: Is it acceptable to be so governed and at that cost?

Foucault's analysis of neoliberalism helps us to conceive of it as a specific art of government which is not good or bad in itself, but which has to be carefully studied if we want to determine how best to comport ourselves towards it, that is, if we want to raise the question of its acceptability, taking advantage of its lines of fragility and blind spots in order to resist (and try to change) what we find unacceptable in it. Indeed, Foucault's perspective on these issues is essentially *strategic* – a perspective that avoids the (simplistic) dichotomy between emancipation and oppression, thus opening the possibility to grasp neoliberal governmentality in its concrete functioning.

A critical (neo)liberalism?

At the beginning of my paper, I raised the following line of argument: Isn't neoliberalism a set of political and economic strategies that give individuals the opportunity to exercise their freedom, allowing them to choose their own personal way of life without coercion? Isn't it a form of governmentality that leaves maximum space for the subject's self-creation and thus effectively facilitates individual difference? And, therefore, doesn't it already comprise a form of *critical force* against domination and discrimination?

In *The birth of biopolitics*, Foucault argues that liberal and neoliberal arts of government fundamentally rely on individual freedom. Instead of interpreting this claim as proof of Foucault's sympathy for or endorsement of neoliberalism, however, we need to combine it with what I have shown so far, remembering that freedom, for Foucault, is not a metaphysical concept, but instead an embodied and specific set of *practices* (Foucault, 1997, pp. 282–284, 300; 2000, pp. 354, 355). Freedom, then, is not to be understood as a condition of perfect and absolute autonomy, nor is it simply an unattainable ideal. It is rather the name for a strategic field of relations that is never stable, but always in motion. As Foucault makes clear several times, the exercise of power in the form of government is

> a set of actions brought to bear upon possible actions; it operates on the field of possibilities in which the behavior of the acting subjects is inscribed: it incites, it induces, it diverts, it makes easier or more difficult, it broadens or restricts, it makes more or less probable. (Foucault, 1982, p. 789)

This means that the notion of government refers specifically to 'the way in which the conduct of individuals or of groups might be directed,' to the attempt to 'structure the possible field of action of others' – their *field of freedom* (p. 790). Therefore, individual freedom always constitutes, according to Foucault, the very condition for the exercise of power, or better, the exercise of the specific form of power Foucault terms 'government': government can only be exercised on free subjects, and only as long as they remain free, that is, as long as they are faced with 'a field of possibilities in which several ways of behaving [*conduites*], several reactions, and diverse comportments, may be realised' (p. 790). In his lectures on *Security, territory, population*, Foucault argues that, starting from the eighteenth century with the *Économistes*,[3] freedom is inserted within governmentality 'not only as the right of individuals legitimately opposed to the power, usurpations, and abuses of the sovereign or the government, but as an element that has become indispensable to governmentality itself' (Foucault, 2007, p. 353). In other words,

> a condition of governing well is that freedom, or certain forms of freedom, are really respected. Failing to respect freedom is not only an abuse of rights with regard to the law, it is above all ignorance of how to govern properly. (p. 353)

Thus, *by definition*, we speak of government (instead of constraint or domination) only insofar as the governed remains to a certain degree *free*.

What is the specificity of neoliberalism in this respect? I would argue that neoliberalism pushes this logic to its limits, attempting to maximise the space of freedom given to (and perceived by) individuals. But this does not imply that neoliberalism is *better* than any other form of governmentality, nor that it is *less dangerous*. Instead, it implies that individual freedom, within a neoliberal rationality of government, becomes *the very instrument* through which individuals are directed. The right question then becomes whether this form of government is *more effective* than others or not. Moreover, as Miguel de Beistegui convincingly shows in his forthcoming book, *The government of desire*, this question also has to be linked to the problem of desire which, in liberal and neoliberal governmentalities, is no longer an *object* of government, as it was before – an object over which the individual needed to exercise a certain control – but an essential *instrument* or *mechanism* of governmentality itself. In other words, the contemporary individual is no longer governed against her own desires; instead, she is governed in the mere fact of the multiplication of her desires in the sphere of the free market: 'From an essentially therapeutic strategy of domination and control,' governmentality moved to 'a strategy of enhancement and maximisation, that is, of management' (de Beistegui, 2016, p. 33). Therefore, desire is now 'integrated as an instrument of government, as that without or against which men cannot be governed': liberal and neoliberal governmentalities are 'the government of desires, by desires, and for desires' (p. 81).

According to Foucault, neoliberalism governs people *through* their freedom because neoliberal governmentality does not only guarantee this or that specific form of freedom: it rather *produces*, *organises*, and *consumes* freedoms. This is why freedom should not be conceived of as 'a universal which is particularised in time and geography,' as 'a white surface with more or less numerous black spaces here and there and from time to time'; instead, freedom is 'an actual relation between governors and governed' (Foucault, 2008, p. 63). If Foucault is right, then in our contemporary neoliberal societies freedom is not (only) something that can be legitimately put in opposition with power, it is not (only) something that power must respect and preserve in order to justify its exercise, but (also and) more fundamentally, freedom is something produced by power itself, or better, by neoliberal technologies of government, and which constitutes the very condition of their existence and functioning. Consequently, we must raise the question of whether claiming a series of individual rights and freedoms in order to protect and increase our field of 'autonomy' is *always*, for us, in this context, an effective way to resist (Cremonesi, Irrera, Lorenzini, & Tazzioli, 2016). Is this claim still capable of engendering, in our contemporary societies, the same *critical* effects it generated a few decades or centuries ago?

This issue is directly connected with another still at the center of contemporary controversies on Foucault's interpretation of neoliberalism: the issue of the so-called 'critical ethos' of liberalism and neoliberalism (Dean & Villadsen, 2016, p. 149). Indeed, in *The birth of biopolitics*, Foucault explicitly defines liberalism – at least in its origins – as a 'critical governmental reason' which raises the problem of 'how not to govern too much': 'a government is never sufficiently aware that it always risks governing too much, or, a government never knows too well how to govern just enough' (Foucault, 2008, pp. 13, 17). Therefore, the liberal art of government seems to be inspired by a *critical ethos*, or the principle of a 'self-limitation of governmental reason' (p. 20). In the Course Summary, Foucault explains:

> Liberalism … is imbued with the principle: 'One always governs too much' – or at least, one should always suspect that one governs too much. Governmentality should not be exercised without a 'critique' far more radical than a test of optimisation. It should not only question itself about the best (or least costly) means for achieving its effects, but also about the possibility and even legitimacy of its project for achieving effects. The question behind the suspicion that there is always the risk of governing too much is: Why, after all, is it necessary to govern? (p. 319)

Geoffroy de Lagasnerie draws from such claims his thesis according to which, in *The birth of biopolitics*, Foucault was interested in highlighting the 'liberatory' or 'emancipatory' character of liberalism and neoliberalism. According to Lagasnerie, inscribed at the heart of these forms of governmentality is a critical force that consists in opposing the state, or better, the *Raison d'État*. Thus, he concludes, Foucault 'perceived neoliberalism as one of the contemporary incarnations of the critical tradition' (de Lagasnerie, 2013, pp. 63, 64). Frédéric Gros, although more prudently, concurs that it is possible to find, in Foucault's work, the thesis according to which, beside political and economic liberalism, there is also something like a 'critical liberalism' which raises the problem of the excess of government (Gros, 2013, p. 42).

While we should not downplay Foucault's definition of liberalism as a principle of restlessness (*'inquiétude'*), of critique addressed to a certain state-centered governmentality (Dean & Villadsen, 2016, p. 148), we should nevertheless be careful to place such a definition in a broader context. Liberalism *can* be considered, at least in its origins, a form of what Foucault calls a 'critical attitude,' or, as he defines it, 'the art of not being governed quite so much' (Foucault, 2015a, p. 37). However, when such a critical interrogation of the excess of government *itself* becomes a mechanism, instrument, or strategy of government – in other words, when the principle of the limitation of government becomes a principle of *self*-limitation that liberal and neoliberal arts of government position at the core of their specific ways of governing human beings – can we legitimately argue that such an interrogation still possesses critical force? Hasn't it simply become an instrument of a new, and more effective, art of government – one that it is possible, and perhaps necessary, to question and criticise *in new ways* (Lorenzini, 2015, p. 71)?

As I have already explained, the freedom claimed by the liberal and neoliberal governmental projects is distinct from a simple juridical status or a space of personal autonomy to be protected against external interferences. In fact, it is also, and more significantly, an effect that has to be produced, incited, and encouraged by these same governmental mechanisms through the formation of a milieu capable of transforming the governed into a receptive and malleable subject without directly constraining her will. This form of freedom, which is often (erroneously) interpreted as the valuable upshot of the liberal and neoliberal critical ethos, is in fact controlled, regulated, and exploited by the liberal and neoliberal arts of government themselves. Therefore, at least in the context of contemporary neoliberal societies, it cannot be considered a form of the critical attitude. It is rather the instrument of a specific form of governmentality (Gros, Lorenzini, Revel, & Sforzini, 2013, p. 8).

As Foucault famously argued in 1984, we must always be suspicious of 'liberation' (since processes of liberation, although sometimes necessary, can easily turn into new forms of domination) and focus instead on the invention of a series of 'practices of freedom' capable of effectively contesting the ways in which we are ordinarily governed (Foucault, 1997, pp. 282, 283). The problem with the liberal principle 'one always governs too much' is precisely that it has largely ceased to play the role of a practice of freedom and has itself become an instrument of government. As a result, it is now legitimate to raise the issue both of its acceptability and the acceptability of neoliberal governmental technologies – along with the question of how to create new forms of the critical attitude and alternate ways of life in contemporary society.

Governable subjects

Since liberalism and neoliberalism are specific ways of governing human beings, it is always possible, and sometimes necessary, to oppose them with the refusal to be governed *like that*. Consequently, the problem of critique and resistance must be reformulated. In fact, if we take seriously Foucault's analyses of liberal and neoliberal governmental technologies as well as his definition of freedom as nothing more (but nothing less) than the *actual* relation between those who govern and the governed, it immediately becomes clear that the demand implicit in an effective practice of resistance in contemporary neoliberal societies can no longer be the demand for *more* freedom. Instead, it must be reconceived as the demand to be governed *differently*, or as the attempt to give a *different* form to one's own subjectivity and life. In other words, the problem is not exactly how to be *more free*, but how to create *alternate forms of subjectivity and life*, that is, alternate ways of establishing relations to oneself and to others, distinct from the kinds of relations encouraged and structured by neoliberal technologies of government.

Critique of and resistance to neoliberal governmentality cannot be detached from an analysis of the concrete forms of subjectivity that such a governmental technology continuously produces through an action on the milieu in which individuals live that relies on their freedom itself. Indeed, Foucault never ceased to insist on the fact that power is not only or essentially repressive; on the contrary, it is productive, and productive of *subjects* (Foucault 1978, p. 94; 1991, p. 194). The *governmental* mechanisms of power, in particular, shape the individual's relations to herself and others down to the minutest detail. In neoliberal governmentality, this process takes the form of the constitution of an entirely new kind of subjectivity: the neoliberal subject is an 'entrepreneur of herself' who tries to effectively manage her natural talents and acquired skills within a space of freedom which seems unlimited. It therefore becomes extremely difficult for her to perceive that this very space of freedom, together with her own subjectivity, are profoundly shaped by neoliberal governmental technologies:

> The society regulated by reference to the market that the neoliberals are thinking about is a society in which the regulatory principle should not be so much the exchange of commodities as the mechanisms of competition. It is these mechanisms that should have the greatest possible surface and depth and should also occupy the greatest possible volume in society. This means that what is sought is not a society subject to the commodity effect, but a society subject to the dynamic of competition. Not a supermarket society, but an enterprise society. The *homo oeconomicus* sought after is not the man of exchange or man the consumer; he is the man of enterprise and production. (Foucault, 2008, p. 147)

The neoliberal art of government creates habits and expectations, shaping behaviors, subjectivities, and ways of living. The form neoliberalism gives to subjectivity, or, more precisely, to the subjectivity of those individuals who are not marginalised and excluded from the beginning (Butler & Athanasiou, 2013, pp. 20, 21; Le Blanc, 2009, pp. 161–191), is not simply that of a subject-consumer, but also that of a subject-entrepreneur who is encouraged to maximise her own 'capital' (consisting not just in one's skills and competencies, but one's genetic inheritance and cultural background as well) in order to be able to compete in the global marketplace (Becker, 1975, pp. 15–80). The more successful the individual is in this endeavor, the more malleable and the more easily and efficiently she is governed. This concept of 'human capital' allows Foucault to reconceptualize the neoliberal constitution of the relations of oneself with oneself and others. The processes of 'internalisation' by the subject of the mechanisms of the market redefine – to a certain extent – the stakes of neoliberal governmentality itself, whose purpose becomes that of extending economic rationality beyond its traditional field of application, with a view to transforming the market not only into a principle of limitation for the state, but also into a mechanism of intelligibility for the whole social field of personal relations (de Beistegui, 2016, pp. 109–117).

According to Gary Becker and the American neoliberals, the theory of human capital is a *new humanism*: to put people at 'the center of the economy' means to conceive of economics not just as a theory of the formation of value, but as an analysis of the rationality of individuals who are free to behave and choose as they wish (Becker, Ewald, & Harcourt, 2012, p. 11). Consequently, since the 1990s, the investment in human capital has become a central element in a discourse 'for the sake of human beings' aiming to reconcile economic performance, social progress, and individual well-being. However, as Luca Paltrinieri rightly observes, it is not possible to ignore that this new humanistic *élan* is furthered by the notion that investing in human capital betters the performance and competitiveness of the neoliberal enterprise. In other words, while human beings are conceived of as ends, they are more fundamentally conceived of as means (Paltrinieri, 2013, pp. 102, 103). Moreover, the definition of human capital as a stock of competencies, modeled on the definition of 'material' capital, is misleading. Competencies, in fact, are never fully acquired, but consist essentially in future possibilities. As a result, they have a *virtual* nature and always stand in need of actualization, since their value cannot be defined in relation to a past or present situation, but only in relation to the flux of revenues they are capable of producing in the future. The neoliberal subject is consequently a *schizophrenic* subject. This schizophrenic condition is precisely that which makes her life precarious and eminently governable: she has to evaluate herself and her stock of competencies here and now, but such an evaluation can only concern future realisations of those competencies (pp. 105, 106). Therefore, the neoliberal subject can enjoy her human capital only in the form of an endless, *precarizing* self-evaluation that should be counted as one of the main strategies of contemporary neoliberal governmentality. As Judith Butler puts it:

> Neoliberal rationality demands self-sufficiency as a moral ideal at the same time that neoliberal forms of power work to destroy that very possibility at an economic level, establishing every member of the population as potentially or actually precarious, even using the ever-present threat of precarity to justify its heightened regulation of public space and its deregulation of market expansion. (Butler, 2015, p. 14)

Foucault never ceased to draw attention to humanistic discourse as a strategy invoked in order to promote economic effectiveness. His analysis in *The birth of biopolitics* is but one more form taken by this critique insofar as it aims to show that the 'free' individual to which the theory of human capital appeals is not a natural, given entity, but a subject *constituted* by neoliberal technologies of government themselves (Golder, 2015, p. 9). Consequently, any mention of a 'critical ethos' in Foucault's work on neoliberalism, I would suggest, should be posited in relation to his attempt to make visible, analyze, and eventually challenge – by means of the creation of *other* forms of subjectivity and life – the concrete processes of subjectivity-constitution that neoliberalism fosters.

Conclusion

In a widely-cited article, Andrew Dilts (2011) argues that it was thanks to his work on neoliberalism that Foucault became interested in the processes of subject-constitution, an interest that would eventually lead him to the study of ancient forms of the care of the self (Foucault, 2005, 2015b). Even though this thesis is highly questionable (Lorenzini, 2013), as the recent publications of Foucault's 1980 lectures at the Collège de France and Dartmouth College have shown (Foucault, 2014, 2015c), it at least has the merit of highlighting the crucial contribution that Foucault's work on neoliberalism can provide to the project of retracing the genealogy of our contemporary form(s) of subjectivity. This project possesses a *critical* dimension that it is important to emphasise in order to question the claim that Foucault's analyses of the ancient care of the self are but a way to 'reinforce' contemporary neoliberal processes of constitution of an eminently governable subject (Nicoli & Paltrinieri, 2017).

Indeed, if it is undeniable that Foucault's work on 'ethics' continues to be extensively cited and utilised in the fields of management and organisational studies (Dean & Villadsen, 2016, p. 6), it comes at the price of a radical de-contextualisation and banalization that transform Foucault's genealogical approach into a ready-made manual for the (entrepreneurial) improvement of oneself. Nothing is further from Foucault's intentions and objectives. Far from presenting an instant 'solution' to the problems of our time, Foucault's late interest in the relations between subjectivity and truth aims to show that our contemporary form(s) of subjectivity are historically, politically, and socially *constructed*, and therefore that they constitute one of the main 'fields of struggle' within which it is possible to fight against neoliberal technologies of government. As a consequence, when Foucault insists, in his analyses of the ancient care of the self, on a series of *technai tou biou* ('arts of living') used by individuals to shape their subjectivity in accordance with objectives radically different from those inscribed at the core of neoliberal rationality, he is not suggesting that we should simply 'reactivate' such techniques. Rather, he is pointing out that it has been historically possible to shape the individual's relations with herself and others in *different ways* – and thus that it is always possible to create new forms of subjectivity and of life (Davidson, 2013). In other words, the notion of an ethics of the care of the self defines, for Foucault, an embodied and contingent set of practices whose ethico-political meaning and strategic significance always have to be appreciated *in context* (Lorenzini, 2015, pp. 265–270).

From this point of view, today, an ethics of the care of the self that does not put at its core the problem of the care received by and offered to others risks being transformed into an instrument of neoliberal governmental strategies rather than a way to resist them. Care ethics (see, e.g., Tronto, 1994) is extremely relevant in this respect, since it emphasises that the notion of an autonomous subject, which is morally and politically valorized but at the same time perpetually put into question by neoliberal forms of power, cannot be made possible for individuals without a whole set of care relations sustaining her life (Laugier, 2018). Thus, by redefining the subject of an ethics of the care of the self on the basis of her essential vulnerability and dependence on others, rather than on her alleged autonomy, we can more readily perceive that the precaritizing nature of the neoliberal processes of subjectivity-constitution needs to be challenged through the elaboration of the 'practices of "communization" of knowledge, mutual aid, and cooperative work' (Dardot & Laval, 2013, p. 321) capable of opening a space for the creation of new forms of subjectivity and life.[4]

The relevance that Foucault's work on neoliberalism and the ancient forms of the relation between subjectivity and truth continues to possess for us today is thus twofold. On the one hand, Foucault's analysis provokes us to reflect on contemporary neoliberal form(s) of subjectivity and of life and to ask ourselves, once it is revealed that they are not natural or given once and for all, whether they are acceptable or unacceptable, dangerous or harmless. On the other hand, Foucault invites us to consider our form(s) of subjectivity and of life as what is most at stake ethically and politically, that is, as realities which are at present profoundly shaped by neoliberal technologies of government, but which, through creative (individual and collective) attempts to shape them *differently*, can also function as strategic practices of freedom.

Notes

1. By 'ethics,' I mean 'the forms of *elaboration* … that one performs on oneself, not only in order to bring one's conduct into compliance with a given rule, but to attempt to transform oneself into the ethical subject of one's behavior' (Foucault, 1985, p. 27). And since one's (everyday) life is the site in which the way one is governed by others is tied to the way she conducts herself (Foucault, 2015c, pp. 25, 26), the processes of subject-constitution and the form(s) taken by one's life are strictly *correlative*. On this point, see Lorenzini, 2015, pp. 10, 11, 88.
2. '[The milieu] is what is needed to account for action at a distance of one body on another. It is therefore the medium of an action and the element in which it circulates. … The milieu is a certain number of combined, overall effects bearing on all who live in it. It is an element in which a circular link is produced between effects and causes, since an effect from one point of view will be a cause from another. … Finally, the milieu appears as a field of intervention in which, instead of affecting individuals as a set of legal subjects capable of voluntary actions – which would be the case of sovereignty – and instead of affecting them as a multiplicity of organisms, of bodies capable of performances, and of required performances – as in discipline – one tries to affect, precisely, a population' (Foucault, 2007, pp. 20, 21).
3. But this is also true, at least in part, for more ancient forms of 'pastoral' governmentality. See Lorenzini, 2016, pp. 15–17.
4. On this point, see also Cukier, 2017, who rightly denounces the exploitation of cooperation under neoliberalism, but who, relying on the concept of alienation, downplays the relevance of the processes of fabrication of a neoliberal form of subjectivity. He therefore underestimates the 'productive' side of neoliberal governmental mechanisms that Foucault's analyses help us to perceive.

Acknowledgments

A version of this paper was given at the international workshop 'The form capitalism gives to our lives' at the Centre Marc Bloch, Berlin, on September 15th–16th, 2016, and at the international conference 'Foucault: Ética e política' at the Universidade da Beira Interior, Covilhã, on March 2nd–3rd, 2017. I am indebted to Alyson Cole, Estelle Ferrarese, Katia Genel, Rahel Jaeggi, Maria Muhle, and the two anonymous reviewers from the *Journal for Cultural Research* for their generous and fruitful comments. I am particularly grateful to Sabina Vaccarino Bremner for her penetrating remarks and invaluable help.

Disclosure statement

No potential conflict of interest was reported by the author.

References

Ball, S. J., & Olmedo, A. (2013). Care of the self, resistance and subjectivity under neoliberal governmentalities. *Critical Studies in Education, 54*(1), 85–96.

Becker, G. S. (1975). *Human capital: A theoretical and empirical analysis, with special reference to education*. New York, NY: National Bureau of Economic Research.

Becker, G. S., Ewald, F., & Harcourt, B. E. (2012). Becker on Ewald on Foucault on Becker: American neoliberalism and Michel Foucault's 1979 Birth of biopolitics lectures. *Institute for Law and Economics Working Paper No. 614/Public Law and Legal Theory Working Paper No. 401*. Retrieved September 23, 2017, from http://chicagounbound.uchicago.edu/cgi/viewcontent.cgi?article=1076&context=law_and_economics

Behrent, M. C. (2009). Liberalism without humanism: Michel Foucault and the free-market creed, 1976–1979. *Modern Intellectual History, 6*(3), 539–568.

Behrent, M. C. (2010). Accidents happen: François Ewald, the 'antirevolutionary Foucault', and the intellectual politics of the French welfare state. *The Journal of Modern History, 82*(3), 585–624.

Butler, J. (2015). *Notes toward a performative theory of assembly*. Cambridge, MA: Harvard University Press.

Butler, J., & Athanasiou, A. (2013). *Dispossession: The performative in the political*. Cambridge: Polity Press.

Cremonesi, L., Irrera, O., Lorenzini, D., & Tazzioli, M. (2016). Foucault and the making of subjects: Rethinking autonomy between subjection and subjectivation. In L. Cremonesi, O. Irrera, D. Lorenzini, & M. Tazzioli (Eds.), *Foucault and the making of subjects* (pp. 1–10), London: Rowman & Littlefield.

Cukier, A. (2017). Entrepreneur de soi ou travailleur aliéné? *Terrains/Théories, 6*. Retrieved September 23, 2017, from http://journals.openedition.org/teth/918

Dardot, P., & Laval, C. (2013). *The new way of the world: On neoliberal society*. London: Verso.

Davidson, A. I. (2013). La fin de l'herméneutique de soi. In D. Lorenzini, A. Revel, & A. Sforzini (Eds.), *Michel Foucault: Éthique et vérité, 1980–1984* (pp. 67–76). Paris: Vrin.

de Beistegui, M. (2016). *The government of desire: A genealogy of the liberal subject*. Chicago, IL: University of Chicago Press (forthcoming; references in the paper are to the unpublished manuscript).

de Lagasnerie, G. (2012). *La dernière leçon de Michel Foucault: Sur le néolibéralisme, la théorie et la politique*. Paris: Fayard.

de Lagasnerie, G. (2013). Néolibéralisme, théorie politique et pensée critique. *Raisons politiques, 52*, 63–76.

Dean, M., & Villadsen, K. (2016). *State phobia and civil society: The political legacy of Michel Foucault*. Stanford, CA: Stanford University Press.

Dilts, A. (2011). From 'entrepreneur of the self' to 'care of the self': Neoliberal governmentality and Foucault's ethics. *Foucault Studies, 12*, 130–146.

Foucault, M. (1978). *The history of sexuality*, Vol. 1. New York, NY: Pantheon Books.

Foucault, M. (1982). The subject and power. *Critical Inquiry, 8*(4), 777–795.

Foucault, M. (1985). *The use of pleasure: Volume 2 of the history of sexuality*. New York, NY: Vintage Books.

Foucault, M. (1991). *Discipline and punish: The birth of the prison*. London: Penguin.

Foucault, M. (1997). The ethics of the concern of the self as a practice of freedom. In *Ethics: Subjectivity and truth* (pp. 281–301). New York, NY: The New Press.

Foucault, M. (2000). Space, knowledge, and power. In *Power* (pp. 349–364). New York, NY: The New Press.

Foucault, M. (2005). *The hermeneutics of the subject: Lectures at the Collège de France, 1981–1982*. Basingstoke: Palgrave Macmillan.

Foucault, M. (2007). *Security, territory, population: Lectures at the Collège de France, 1977–1978*. Basingstoke: Palgrave Macmillan.

Foucault, M. (2008). *The birth of biopolitics: Lectures at the Collège de France, 1978–1979*. Basingstoke: Palgrave Macmillan.

Foucault, M. (2014). *On the government of the living: Lectures at the Collège de France, 1979–1980*. Basingstoke: Palgrave Macmillan.

Foucault, M. (2015a). Qu'est-ce que la critique? In *Qu'est-ce que la critique? suivi de La culture de soi* (pp. 33–70). Paris: Vrin.

Foucault, M. (2015b). La culture de soi. In *Qu'est-ce que la critique? suivi de La culture de soi* (pp. 81–98). Paris: Vrin.

Foucault, M. (2015c). *About the beginning of the hermeneutics of the self: Lectures at Dartmouth College, 1980*. Chicago, IL: University of Chicago Press.

Golder, B. (2015). *Foucault and the politics of rights*. Stanford, CA: Stanford University Press.

Gros, F. (2013). Y a-t-il un sujet biopolitique? *Nóema, 4*(1), 31–42.

Gros, F., Lorenzini, D., Revel, A., & Sforzini, A. (2013). Introduction au dossier 'Les néolibéralismes de Michel Foucault'. *Raisons politiques, 52*, 5–11.

Laugier, S. (2018). Politics of vulnerability and responsibility for ordinary others. In E. Ferrarese (Ed.), *The politics of vulnerability* (pp. 57–73). New York, NY: Routledge.

Le Blanc, G. (2009). *L'invisibilité sociale*. Paris: PUF.

Lorenzini, D. (2013). Dall'ermeneutica del sé alla politica di noi stessi. *Nóema, 4*(1), 1–10.

Lorenzini, D. (2015). *Éthique et politique de soi: Foucault, Hadot, Cavell et les techniques de l'ordinaire*. Paris: Vrin.

Lorenzini, D. (2016). From counter-conduct to critical attitude: Michel Foucault and the art of not being governed quite so much. *Foucault Studies, 21*, 7–21.

Nicoli, M., & Paltrinieri, L. (2017). Du management de soi à l'investissement sur soi: Remarques sur la subjectivité post-néo-libérale. *Terrains/Théories, 6*. Retrieved September 23, 2017, from https://teth.revues.org/929

Paltrinieri, L. (2013). Quantifier la qualité: Le 'capital humain' entre économie, démographie et éducation. *Raisons politiques, 52*, 89–107.

Taylan, F. (2013). L'interventionnisme environnemental, une stratégie néolibérale. *Raisons politiques, 52*, 77–87.

Tronto, J. C. (1994). *Moral boundaries: A political argument for an ethic of care*. New York, NY: Routledge.

Zamora, D. (2014). Can we criticize Foucault? *Jacobin*. Retrieved September 23, 2017, from https://www.jacobinmag.com/2014/12/foucault-interview/

8 The subject of objects

Marx, new materialism, & queer forms of life

Alyson Cole

ABSTRACT
This article examines two interrelated themes in the scholarship categorized as 'new materialism': first, the aim to undermine the subject/object distinction; second, the proposition that agency exists across the material world. While new materialists, such as Jane Bennett, conceive of their approach as an intervention against the injurious effects of capitalism, I argue that destabilizing the object/subject binary and endowing inanimate objects with vitality and agency is actually a constitutive feature of capitalism itself. To illustrate this point, I turn to Marx's analysis, providing a queer reading of his theorization of commodities. Revisting Marx's account of commodity fetishism in tandem with new materialism yields fresh insights into the logics of capitalism, specifically, the manner in which it thrives on concurrently producing and erasing subjectivities, thereby distorting social materiality and material sociality.

A growing field in political theory casts material things as vital to preserving democracy, or as vital in themselves. There is, we are told, 'thing power,' and learning to be attuned to the agency of matter matters to addressing our most urgent problems, from the destructive circulation of global capital and entwining population flows, to escalating threats posed by anthropocentric climate change and the rapid proliferation of new technologies. 'Accepting the otherness of things,' one writer proffers, 'is the condition for accepting otherness as such' (Brown, 2001, p. 12). These 'new materialists' draw from a range of scholarship across various disciplines. The philosophies of Spinoza and Deleuze, in addition to theories from science and technology studies have had an unmistakable impact, as have recent discoveries in the natural sciences (neurology, biology and physics in particular) that further demonstrate that matter is neither inert nor discrete, and does not adhere to linear cause and effect (Knappett & Malafouris, 2008, p. xiv). Such work invites reassessing the entire 'edifice of modern ontology regarding notions of change, causality, agency, time [,] … space' and life itself (Coole & Frost, 2010, pp. 9, 24). In rising to this challenge, new materialists dispense with cultural, constructivist, semiotic, or linguistic approaches employing instead 'methodological realism' (Ibid., p. 25). 'Language has been granted too much power,' Karen Barad boldly asserts; or, as Manuel DeLanda frames it, we need to 'put language last' (Barad, 2003, p. 801; Delanda,

2006, p. 16). Putting materiality first, these scholars conceive of inorganic matter as possessing fecund and inventive capacities. 'Materiality is always something more than "mere" matter: an excess, force, vitality, relationality or difference that renders matter active, self-creative, productive and unpredictable.' Indeed, matter no longer is, 'matter becomes' (Coole & Frost, 2010, p. 9).

If everything, human and nonhuman, animate and inanimate, natural and artifactual, has agentic capacities, self-organization, self-directedness, willfulness and recalcitrance, agency can no longer be conceived of in distinctly human terms of intentionality and choice. It is rather an 'event' in which a variety of forces – bodily functions, affective reactions, electromagnetic fields, and an assortment of objects – interact in an 'assemblage.' 'This is not a world … of subjects and of objects, but of various materialities constantly engaged in a network of relations' (Bennett, 2004, p. 354). In turn, post-humanist politics becomes thoroughly open-ended, an ever-present possibility for incremental experimentation (Connolly, 2013, pp. 399–412).

This article focuses on two aspects of the new materialist project: first, the aim to undermine, or eradicate, the subject/object distinction; second, and relatedly, the conception of agency as distributed across the material world, thereby eliminating conceptual (often hierarchical) distinctions that differentiate humans from their environments. While new materialists understand their approach as intervening against the injurious effects of late capitalism, I argue that destabilizing the object/subject binary and endowing inanimate objects with agentic vitality is actually a constitutive feature of capitalism itself. To illustrate this point, I turn to Marx's analysis of how capitalism forms and deforms life and things, especially his foundational theorizing about commodities. My purpose is not to dismiss the 'new materialist turn' as the most recent iteration of commodity fetishism, however. Revisting Marx's historical materialism in tandem with new materialism yields fresh insights into the logics of capitalism, specifically, the manner in which capitalism thrives on concurrently producing and erasing subjectivities, and its proclivity (through the power of abstraction) to distort our social materiality and material sociality.

Capitalism generates a series of oppositions. It 'generalizes in every domain the structure of separation,' Agamben observes, 'a … ceaseless process of separation that assails every thing, every place, every human activity in order to divide it from itself … even the human body, even sexuality, even language' (Agamben, 2007, p. 81). Such splitting reorganizes our way of life through inversions and displacements. While these sharply delineated binaries are well accounted for in the dense corpus of Marxian interpretation, their inherent instability is less often accentuated. Interlacing with these divisions, capitalism additionally requires that we occupy two subject positions (sometimes alternatively, at other times concurrently) as desiring subjects and/or docile objects. It forms, on the one hand, the subjectivity of consumers (typically as gendered members of the modern, market-oriented nuclear family). On the other hand, workers are dehumanized and objectified for the purpose of extracting labor power and surplus value. Objects follow a similar trajectory – commodified as complete, autonomous entities, but in the process they somehow additionally assume a life (or subjectivity) 'of their own.'

This essay begins by retreading some rather familiar ground, namely, Marx's historical materialism and his analysis of the commodity form. I am attentive to opacities in his theorizing, ambiguities reflected in disagreements among his many distinguished interpreters. I then turn to the new materialist literature and its relationship to Marx's theories, concentrating on the work of one innovator in the field, Jane Bennett. I conclude by returning to Marx to trouble his evocative assertion that the commodity form is 'queer' (*vertrackt*). While Marx used the term merely as an adjective to denote the peculiar process of capitalist commodification and our relationship to it (and some translators opt for other English adjectives), I reread his theory in line with current uses of 'queer' as a verb.[1] Reading Marx queerly amplifies, beyond the multivalence of his text, new possibilities for calling into question not just the commodity as a form but as a form of life that warps our intersubjective materiality.

The commodity form

Marx insists on the historical specificity of the material relationship of actors and their activities. In contrast to Feuerbach's metaphysical materialism, he grounded his materialism in the human body, its engagement with other human bodies and nature, and the specific tools such bodies use. These are the elements that determine how individuals express and produce their 'definite mode of life' (Marx & Engels, 1970, p. 42).[2] Ridiculing political economists for universalizing categorically capitalist modes of production and exchange, he explains that the exploitative and coercive social relations inherent to capitalism seem natural and necessary only because they appear to assume a material form (Marx, 1976, pp. 148–151, 168). In the *Manuscripts*, Marx clarifies how capitalist production alienates workers from their natural environment, their ability to work, the products of their labor, and their 'species being.' By objectifying their labor and selling it on the market, '*man himself* becomes the object' (Marx, 1974, p. 95). Workers only work to live and live to work, and increasingly their labor diminishes rather than fulfills them. 'Labor produces not only commodities; it produces itself and the worker as a commodity' (Marx, 1974, p. 63). As workers are degraded to the status of things, the products of their labor assume an elevated status as independently powerful, 'autonomous figures endowed with a life of their own' (1976, p. 165). Whereas the *Manuscripts* explicated the objectification of labor and laborers, in the fourth section of the first chapter of *Capital* Marx describes the subjectification of objects, a dynamic he calls 'commodity fetishism.'[3]

Commodities are multivalent things. As 'objects of utility' they possess 'use value,' but also represent 'exchange value,' the social relationship between things – not between humans or between humans and the product of their labor (1976, pp. 126–128). Commodities become the bond connecting people, obscuring human relations even as they structure them. Divorced from their utility and the labor invested in their production, objects seem to possess properties that are neither inherent nor material. The capitalist form of life materializes objects as subjects – commodities and all forms of capital – so that they possess a 'phantom-like objectivity' (Marx, 1976, p. 128).

According to several of Marx's interpreters, this account of commodity fetishism in *Capital* aptly characterizes the entirety of life under capitalism, where anything and everything can be commodified and affective attachments are to objects rather than one another. 'Commodity relations tend to make people view others instrumentally rather than intersubjectively and to induce people to enter into personal and emotional relations with things' (Foley, 1986, p. 29). Georg Lukács famously deemed the fetishism of commodities, or 'reification,' to be Marx's fundamental insight into the structural problem of capitalist society 'in all its aspects' (1971, p. 170). Issak Illich Rubin similarly counseled against relegating Marx's discussion of commodity fetishism to some sociological flourish, tangential to his critique of political economy. It was, rather, the linchpin of his work; though he complained, 'Marx was very stingy in his remarks on the theory of fetishism' (Rubin, 2008, p. 55).

Lukács and Rubin, among others, therefore understand Marx's account of commodity fetishism as seamlessly extending and refining his earlier writings about alienation, a critique of capitalism that reaches beyond market or economic relations to all aspects of life. Marx, they maintain, demystifies the value of commodities in *Capital* order to provide the insights necessary to dispel a collective misperception.[4]

> [A]ll the mystifications of the capitalist mode of production, all capitalism's illusions about freedom, all the apologetic tricks of vulgar economists, have as their basis the form of appearance … which makes the actual relation invisible, and indeed presents to the eye the precise opposite of that relation (1976, p. 680).

The value of commodities derives from human labor and exits only in the context of human needs; all the rest is capitalist chicanery.

New, old & vital materialism

The designation 'new materialism' covers a broad range of scholarship with differing foci (objects and things, materialism and object-oriented ontologies) and employs various cognates (matter, mattering, materiality, materialization).[5] New materialists coin new vocabularies and radically rework central concepts, beginning with materiality itself. Matter in their texts typically becomes less an object than a process. 'Matter does not refer to a fixed substance; rather matter is substance in its intra-active becoming – not a thing, but a doing, a congealing of agency,' explains Karen Barad (2003, p. 822). Correspondingly, they turn their attention to bodies, human and non-human – flesh, bacteria, and all forms of matter, whether natural or artifactual. Such a wide-ranging understanding of materiality undermines a host of traditional dualisms (e.g. mind/body or mind/matter, culture/nature, human/nonhuman).

New materialists clearly have an ambivalent relationship with Marx and 'old' materialism more generally. On the one hand, most scholars present their work as a critical intervention into the destructive material practices that sustain systems of international capitalism, and, in turn, contribute to climate change, global inequality and warfare, rendering some lives livable and others disposable (Coole & Frost, 2010, p. 30; Edwards, 2010, pp. 296–297). Their engagement with matter, however expansively defined, could be seen as building upon Marx's grounding of metaphysical materialism, especially his efforts to denaturalize social, historically contingent modes of life, and demonstrate the entwinement of culture and materiality (Edwards, 2010, pp. 282–283, 285).[6] From this perspective, new materialism need not be incompatible with historical materialism. As Kathy Ferguson configures the relationship between new and old materialism, 'the new materialism does not replace the old, but leaves room for it while directing attention to a different register of human relations with the other-than-human world' (Ferguson, 2013, p. 17).

On the other hand, many new materialists explicitly position their work as a radical departure from previous understandings of materialism and Marx in particular. Pheng Cheah, to give one example, dismisses Marx's theories as 'irrigated by an ontology of organismic vitalism' (2010, p. 71). She finds fault with his reliance on Hegelian negation, consciousness, and human activity (specifically labor) as the force driving teleologically structured movement.

Such anthropocentric resonances in Marx's work would seem to foreclose the possibility of 'nonhumanity to appear on the ethical radar screen,' and accordingly, most new materialists reject it (Bennett, 2004, p. 357).

'It is important that "materiality" be a contested term in political theory,' Bennett asserts, 'especially as it replaces "reality" as the name for the stuff to which theory must be tied if it is to make a difference' (Ibid., p. 366). Allowing for such contestation, Bennett sometimes presents her 'vital materialism' as 'parallel' to historical materialism, seeing the latter as focused on the economic and the former as understanding matter more capaciously – as 'bona fide agents rather than…instrumentalities, technics of power, recalcitrant objects or social constructs' (2010a, p. 47). At other times, she casts her project as a 'competitor alongside' Marx's materialism (Bennett, 2004, pp. 348, 366). Either way, Bennett unequivocally maintains that matter has autonomous agentic capacities. It is not simply that matter acts upon us, serves to orient, creates proximities or obstacles, enables and disables. She insists that inanimate things have the ability 'to animate, to act, to produce effects dramatic and subtle' (2010a, p. 6). She calls her approach 'thing-power materialism': 'the capacity of things … to act as quasi agents or forces with trajectories, propensities, or tendencies of their own' (Ibid., p. vii). The vitality of objects exceeds the contexts in which we try to place them, and is 'never entirely exhausted by their semiotics' (2004, p. 351).

As against the Weberian narrative of disenchanted modernity and the iron cage of bureaucratic rationality, Bennett offers 'onto-stories' of escape, excess, irrationality, and boundless possibilities for enchantment. Through a 'strategic anthromorphism' she aims to inspire her reader to be 'struck and shaken by the extraordinary that lives amid the familiar and everyday' (2010b, p. 99, 2001, p. 4). In doing so, she hopes to incite alternative sensibilities, different aesthetic dispositions, and new emotional attachments, all of which she maintains will enable us to assume the 'generous mood' necessary to develop an affective posture of connectedness to nature and the world of things (2010a, pp. 149, 156). After all, fostering joy is as important to politics as indignation, she reasons, for it provides the energy to fight against injustice (2010b, p. 38, 2001, p. 128).

Given how central 'commodification' is to a Marxian lexicon and the critique of consumerism more generally, we might expect that commodities would be absent from the things that new materialists include in their account of matter, especially such a joy-filled one as Bennett's. The language of commodification usually denotes something negative, while 'object,' 'thing,' and 'matter' allow for more ambiguous meanings. Bennett, however, explicitly extends her analysis to include commodities. Our consumerist practices, even our susceptibility to commercialization and privatized attachments to specific commodities, she embraces as modes of enchantment too. She writes effusively and extensively about the 'aesthetic of vibrant mobility' of a 1998 televised GAP ad for khaki trousers. 'Out of the commercialized dance erupts a kind of neo-Pagan or Epicurean materialism – an enchanted materialism' (2001, p. 118). The sort of advertisements run by this 16-billion-dollar corporation, she contends, might motivate 'ethically useful' allure, in addition to propelling viewers to purchase new clothes.

Contra Marx's account of commodity fetishism and Adorno and Horkheimer's critiques of the 'culture industry,' Bennett stakes out a more ambivalent position. True, excessive consumerism produces abundant waste and relies on exploitative labor relations, but there might be liberatory potential in consumptive practices as well (Ibid., pp. 129, 113). Since we will never be commodity-free, the real question is how to reform commodity culture. Her answer: embrace the power of commodities; that 'sense of vitality, the charged-up feeling often generated in human bodies by the presence of the promise of commodity consumption' (Ibid., p. 14). The somatic charge derived from spending money (even frivolously), the pleasure of ownership ('affective energetics of consumption'), she analogizes to 'moral sentiments' that likewise can propel ethical action (Ibid., pp. 124, 114). Rationalist demystification is not enough to nurture the ethic of care, in part because it reduces '*political* agency to *human* agency' (2010a, p. xv, emphasis in original). What Marx and his fellow travelers fail to recognize is that their analyses deprive us of the resources that motivate political change – namely, 'the idealism and somatic will' – by undermining the few possibilities of elation (however derived) available under capitalism (2001, p. 130).

In line with Deleuze's theories, Bennett doubts that capitalism is as efficient and totalizing as Marxian thinkers hold (Ibid., p. 116). She views her work as identifying 'lines of flight' within the system. Marx remains too focused on the harm commodification enacts on humans, and he is too quick to denounce animism as fetishistic, she explains. In her account, Marx's analysis of commodity fetishism represents a reductive diagnostic classification of a 'perceptual disorder' (Ibid., p. 113).

She also takes aim at the term 'fetish,' condemning it as colonialist racism. This is a long-standing criticism. Jean Baudrillard, among many others, likewise troubled the origins of the concept in rationalistic Occidental Christianity and humanism, though he considered recourse to fetishism less an offense than a 'short-circuited' analysis of a deeper phenomenon, obscuring 'consummativity' (1981, p. 88). (Tongue in cheek, he remarks that we have a conceptual fetish about fetishism!)[7] The imprint of Charles de Brosses's *The Cult of Fetish God* (1760/1989) is questionably evident in *Capital* as well as several of Marx's earlier writings.[8] In all these contexts 'fetishism' denotes mystification on par with religion, and of course Marx uses the term to criticize religiosity itself.[9]

Queer secrets

While scholars parse the term 'fetish,' there is another keyword in the title of this section of *Capital* that merits attention – 'The fetishism of commodities and the *secret* thereof.' What secret does Marx reveal? One common interpretation is our fetishism; we are unaware of our primal attachments to things. Fetishizing the commodity erases from both individual and social consciousness its materiality, and thus it remains profoundly potent and yet invisible, unknown. At the same time, the commodity itself encapsulates a secret, since it veils social relations, flattening and homogenizing qualitatively different forms of labor to one value-form. It thus contains the hidden key to the capitalist economy in its entirety: the contradiction of value versus price. One secret, in other words, conceals another.

Grasping Marx's full meaning requires shifting our attention from the question of fetishism to the logic of secrets. Disclosing secrets is integral to the intellectual work that Marx performs. Indeed, he shrouds the commodity in additional layers of mystery. His analysis estranges the commodity by questioning the givenness of the given, exposing the artificiality of what is presumed to be natural, and thus disrupting normative strictures. As he writes, '[The commodity's] *analysis* shows that it is, in reality, a very queer (*vertrackt*) thing' (Marx and Engels 1996, p. 81, emphasis added). Marx thus queers the commodity in two ways: first, through analytically underscoring the entwinement of visibility and invisibility, a dialectic we associate today with the epistemology of the closet; second, and more radically, by suggesting that capitalism altered the ontological boundaries distinguishing subjects and objects, life and nonlife.

This is not the only time Marx has promised his readers to divulge secrets. Clandestine silences abound in the *Grundrisse*, for example, from the deceptions of Proudhist's thinking to the terms of government loans.[10] Nevertheless, in *Capital*, Marx lays bare his findings in a distinct way. For in this text things dance, spin around, turn upside down, and talk, or at least Marx ventriloquizes the commodity doing so.

> Could commodities themselves speak, they would say: Our use value may be a thing that interests men. It is no part of us as objects. What, however, does belong to us as objects, is our value. Our natural intercourse as commodities proves it. In the eyes of each other we are nothing but exchange values (1996, pp. 93–94).

Even as he criticizes how capitalism elevates objects into subjects, Marx anthropomorphizes commodities by endowing them with voice, perspective and agency. He actually scripts a doubled ventriloquy, for after telling us what commodities would say he contrives a response from economists.

Capital otherwise is a book notorious for numerous lengthy passages of dense prose, filled with equations, formulas, and rather tedious accounting. The chapter on 'The Working Day' is exemplary in this regard. Marx was well aware of the burden his tome imposed on readers, and concedes as much in the preface to the French edition (1872), where he cautions that his text, especially in the first chapters, 'makes for somewhat arduous reading' (Marx and Engels 1996, p. 23). Almost apologetically he explains that the scientific method necessitates such demanding formulations of ideas and evidence, promising that the rewards will match his readers' efforts. The section on the fetishism of commodities differs in this respect. Some even consider it the epitome of Marx's rhetorical embellishment, on par with 'imaginative literature,' 'a dramatic poem, or possibly a dramatic epic' (Hyman, 1962, p. 133; Sypher, 1948, p. 438).

The placement of the section on commodity fetishism in the text is rather queer too, a curious disruption to the arc of his argument. Both Althusser and Balibar remark that Marx's account of commodity fetishism appears too early in the text to advance his theory. They consider it premature for Marx to explicate the meaning of value and money in the first chapter of Volume One before he has elaborated on the capitalist mode of production (Althusser, 2006; Balibar, 2014). Employing such literary devices, ostensibly cloaking the already enigmatic with additional abstruseness, would be counterproductive if Marx's primary purpose was simply to demystify commodities.

What of the ambiguities in the analysis itself? Marx opens the section about commodity fetishism by informing readers that he will state the obvious, accounting for something relatively simple, even banal ('a very trivial thing, and easily understood'). Conversely, he also writes that he will need to decipher the undecipherable, comparing the commodity form to a 'social hieroglyphic' necessitating decoding. Straightforward translation apparently will not suffice, since 'to stamp an object of utility as a value is just as much a social product as language' (Marx and Engels 1996, p. 85). Because they speak a language specific to their form of life, commodities must be extracted from the depths of the capitalist closet and incited to speak.

Casting the commodity as a secret steeped in metaphysical complexities challenges our understanding of commodities across the object/subject, epistemological/ontological, and life/nonlife divides. Marx's talking commodity is, I propose, analytically significant to his argument, rather than merely a sardonic device to ridicule atavistic fetishism. Instead, Marx wants us to understand that secrets captivate us because of the power they conceal. His injunction to make commodities share their secret in some ways foreshadows Foucault's study of the economy of exchange and desire.[11] The dynamics of the 'open secret' Foucault outlines in the *History of Sexuality* parallels the logic of the commodity form – a paradoxical fusing of the visibility of the supposedly invisible, of ceaselessly speaking about the unspeakable, 'whose discovery is imperative, a thing abusively reduced to silence, and at the same time difficult and necessary, dangerous and precious to divulge' (1978, pp. 34–35). Note also that Foucault suggests that agency is mistakenly attributed to that concealment (Ibid., p. 151). Commodities in Marx's account, like sex in Foucault's, effectively cloak their respective vulnerable foundations as formations, as forms.

Rather than anachronistically reading Foucault into Marx, however, we might instead take his queer text at face value, subjecting it to the sort of 'surface reading' the anti-fetishists prefer. For even if the fetishism of commodities resembles a repressed secret that needs to be liberated from the capitalist closet, the more troubling aspect of the commodity form is its role in capitalism's creatively destructive circuits; how capitalism thoroughly and profoundly distorts material sociality by generating new life forms that defy existing categories, since commodities reside somewhere between life/nonlife (or organic/inorganic). To pursue this line of interpretation we might begin by placing Marx's account of capitalism in the context of various 19th century literary depictions of industrial urbanity or capitalism in general; for instance, Charles Dickens's famous portrayal of Manchester in *Hard Times* (1854) as a menacing jungle in which wild, monstrous animals are supplanted by dreadful, smoke-bellowing factories ready to devour life, or H.G. Wells's horrifying *Island of Dr. Moreau* (1896) inhabited by repugnant creatures produced by fusing different species.

Since the publication of Derrida's *Specters of Marx* (1993), studies of the spectral in Marx's writing have proliferated. Scholars pursue the theme and imagery of the phantasmal and monstrous in his work, especially Marx's frequent metaphoric use of Gothic figures, such as vampires and werewolves, to underscore capitalists' insatiable desire for accumulation, as well as how capitalist production inverts and perverts social relations, perhaps most profoundly the 'rule of things over men, of dead labor over living' (Marx 1976, pp. 342, 989–990). Through these metaphors Marx augments how capitalism robs workers of their humanity or 'sensuousness,' pointing to permutations of the natural/supernatural, sensuous life/living dead. Still, Marx's analysis of the commodity itself evokes not the living dead as much as how capitalism confers agency and life on material forms that were never alive. To put it differently, the trouble with commodification is less the perversion of bios than the birth of alternative and distinctly nonhuman forms of life.

Prosaically real

As we have seen, the life attributed to commodities can be understood as a product of misrecognition, a cognitive error, as several of Marx's interpreters claim. By employing the language of estrangement, Marx seeks to unshackle his readers' belief system from its stubborn ideological moorings, pushing the metaphor of the religious fetish ad absurdum. Anthropomorphizing commodities in his text would then be primarily a rhetorical device deployed to call into question perceptions ingrained in false consciousness, namely, the vital role of commodities in the capitalist imaginary.

At the same time, the world that capitalism created may be grossly distorted, but it is nonetheless real, not just trickery and smoke screens that can be readily exposed and chased away. Under capitalism, the products of workers' labor do, in fact, regulate their lives, sculpting and perverting life itself. In this sense commodity power is empirical, 'prosaically real, and by no mean imaginary mystification' (Marx, 1981, p. 49). Individuals living in capitalist society correctly perceive the power of this form: '[T]o the producers ... the social relations between their private labors *appear as what they are*, i.e. they do not appear as direct social relations between persons in their work, but rather as material relations between things' (Marx 1976, p. 166). The fetishism of commodities cannot, therefore, be adequately understood as a diagnostic classification referring to a 'perceptual disorder,' a delusion, or false consciousness. Nor is Marx identifying an inversion that needs only to be exposed and turned right side up. The life of commodities is far more complicated. Precisely because it is not solely an optical, perceptual or epistemological error, addressing commodity fetishism entails more than altering ideas.[12]

Marx's understanding of the 'prosaically real' foundations of capitalist relations lies less in the subject/object dynamic than in the form itself. Rancière guides us toward this reading when he observes that what is distinctive about Marx's conceptualization of commodity fetishism in *Capital* is the absence of a subject, which he reads as a departure from the sort of 'anthropological causality' and conceptualization of the subject/object Marx employed in the *Manuscripts*.[13]

> The terms present are not subject, predicate, and things, but relation and form. The becoming alien in question here does not mark the externalization of the predicates of a subject in an alien entity, but designates what becomes of the relations of capital in the most mediated form of the process...the social determinations of the relations of production will thus find themselves reduced to the material determinations of the thing (Rancière, 2015, pp. 156–157).

Even if it is not inherent in the 'coarse materiality of their substance,' the commodity form, as embedded in everyday practices and institutions, is an ontological formulation, not primarily an epistemological one.

Queering the commodity opens an indeterminate space where humans assume the status of objects and objects acquire characteristics approximating subjectivity. The epistemic error that Marx uncovers, the false consciousness engendered by the commodity form, does not emanate from a misperception of 'objective reality' but from the misconception of that reality as natural, necessary, transhistorical, and universal. Our current form of life, the social conventions produced and reproduced by capitalism, leads us to take for granted what we should not. '[F]etishism is not a subjective phenomenon or a false perception of reality, as an optical illusion or a superstitious belief would be,' Balibar submits. 'It constitutes, rather the way in which reality...cannot but appear' (2014, p. 60). Our perceptions of commodities may be flawed, but they are not false. In *Capital* Marx endeavors to explain the structure of capitalism's social relations and production – capital's biopolitics – not to establish the veracity of the role of commodities in our lives.

Weber argues that capitalism disenchants the world, whereas Marx makes clear that capitalism in fact also enchants modern life through certain forms of materialization and abstraction. Perhaps most miraculous of all is money; it magically transforms any number of impairments, incapacities and character failings 'into their contrary' (Marx, 1974, p. 121). Whereas commodification conceals the originary labor that created the object, money hides nothing. It has no value outside the exchange; it is 'the perversion and objectification of production relations in their highest degree' (Marx, 2000, p. 522). The commodity form masks human relations even as it structures them, but capital, especially interest bearing capital, obliterates the pretense of any relations (whether between humans, humans and objects, or objects themselves). Its agency defines the apex of commodification, since money is self-generating: 'an automaton, of creating surplus-value in geometrical progression …' (Marx, 2000, p. 531). The image of money as 'pregnant in itself,' an unproductive reproductivity, highlights the irregularity of this form of life.

The commodity form as a 'form of life'

The commodity form situates the commodity in a liminal terrain between life and non-life. Its life, in other words, its agency, autonomy, and vitality are accentuated as it always flirts with extinction. There is the risk, for instance, that the commodity's materiality will escape its form, on account of either its own vulnerability as a destructible object or because the underlying social relations will surface, call attention to themselves, and somehow diffuse the magic. Moreover, objects move in and out of the commodity form; their life trajectory as a commodity can also be eventful, prone to the powers of time, space, and the ever-changing nature of fashion, taste, culture in general, as well as the instabilities of both its use and exchange values.[14]

Marx goes to great lengths to distinguish between the materiality of the commodity and its form, as we have seen. The commodity/life nexus is a complex foregrounding of the idea that agency and vitality are conditional, situated, and constructed. It is tempting, therefore, to view these aspects of Marx's analysis as precursor to new materialism, irrespective of the efforts of many of these scholars to distance themselves from his approach. And yet, what remains crucial in Marx's account of the commodity is not its agency as much as its passing nature and distance/separation from the material world. The same might apply to conventional or biological life-forms since the terms 'agency,' 'vitality' and 'life' are value-laden, normatively ideological, and not, therefore, ingrained in matter. New materialism itself engages in metaphysical reasoning to the extent that their project entails assigning nonmaterial, normative attributes such as agency and vitality to inanimate objects.

The mechanisms new materialists deploy to destabilize conventional categories of political thought differ substantially and are more far-reaching than Marx's formulation of capitalism, as is the manner in which they attribute agency to all matter rather than simply commodities. Moreover, new materialists' efforts not only to correct a misunderstanding of materiality, but also to cultivate a certain respect and deference towards nonhuman life and matter is quite important. Bennett, for instance, rightly identifies unbridled hubris grounded in the conception of matter as inanimate and dead as an obstacle to formulating more sustainable modes of production and consumption (2010a, p. ix). In this regard, 'antimateriality' aptly captures what fuels hyperconsumption and excessive waste (Ibid., p. 5).

At the same time, the promiscuous and universal allocation of life, in some permutations of new materialist theory, obscures other manifestations of capitalist injustice. If everything is agentic, if causality and responsibility are always diffused and dispersed, then the entrenched, often static, hierarchies within at least human society disappear from view. In attempting to undermine the destructiveness of human sovereignty and to find political significant in the flux of matter, new materialists seem to occlude how social, economic and political inequalities are tied to positions that reproduce and sustain themselves despite the constant circulation of capital.

While capitalism thrives on the production of divisions, it concurrently requires the dissolution of boundaries, including those that differentiate and juxtapose subjects and objects. Capitalism generates nonhuman, non-biological forms of life, to the extent that it bestows agency, coherence, and autonomy on objects through the process of commodification. New materialism's aim to dissolve the object/subject dyad by amplifying the agency of matter may have transgressive, even transformative potential. Nonetheless, we need to remember that, historically, undermining the boundaries separating objects and subjects and approaching objects' life form have been crucial to capitalist destruction and dehumanization of all forms of life. How new materialists' *vital* insights might be modified to better address these problematic affinities is a question that merits additional consideration.

Notes

1. The *Flügel–Schmidt–Tanger* dictionary offers the following English synonyms for *vertrackt*: 'distorted, deformed; intricate; odd, strange, queer; desperate; confounded, devilish' (Schmidt and Tanger 1913, p. 898). See also Baumann (1931), p. 1059.
2. Marx does not use the term '*Lebensform*', but instead '*Lebensweise*' (roughly translated as 'a way of life'). While semantically similar, and thus some scholars consider the terms synonymous; others argue that they are importantly different. Cf. Hacker (2013).
3. Note that Rubin (2008) claims that in the original German edition the entire first chapter, including the fetishism segment, was one general section entitled 'Commodities.'
4. Baudrillard (1981), although from a critical perspective, also views Marx's reference to fetishism as depicting false consciousness. He reasons that Marx retains a notion of true consciousness (i.e. use-value) and thus 'eliminates any real chance [he] has of analyzing the actual process of ideological labor' (p. 89). 'The term "fetishism" almost has a life of its own,' Baudrillard continues, '... it turns against those who use it, and surreptitiously exposes their own magical thinking' (p. 90).
5. Of course, material culture as a focus of study has a longer lineage in cultural studies and anthropology. Cf., e.g., Appadurai (1986).
6. Even as Marx emphasized the role of the relations of production, he recognized that needs, 'habits and expectations,' vary in different cultures, however much the market might manipulate them. Some new materialists likewise amplify the role of capitalist production and consumption in materializing life. Cf. Edwards (2010).
7. The term dates back to the 16th century and has since been employed in a variety of contexts with varied meanings – psychoanalysis (Freud), anthropology (Comte), religious studies (de Brosse), and more recently queer theory. In most uses, 'fetish' expresses 'a concern with how an object comes to be seen as an active force that has some power-effect on subjects' (Heatherington, 2007, p. 52). And, further, that the power of the object is illusory: it is not what it seems to be, it disguises, distorts, perverts and displaces. But see Mulvey (1996).
8. Before *Capital*, Marx used the term 'fetish' to challenge Hermes's religious defense of the Prussian state (1842), German wood theft laws (1842), and Europeans' preoccupation with gold (1844).
9. In rejecting Marx's account of commodity fetishism Bennett extends a Latourian 'factish' anti-fetishism, a repudiation of critical theory in general for engaging in 'critical barbarity' on materiality and for being engaged by 'matters of concern, not matters of fact' (Latour 2004, p. 231; See also Latour 1999, 2011).
10. 'The concept of value is entirely peculiar to the most modern economy, since it is the most abstract expression of capital itself and of the production resting on it. In the concept of value its secret is betrayed ... the economic concept of value does not occur in antiquity' (Marx, 1993, pp. 776–777).
11. For a thoughtful analysis linking the logics of queer desire and the commodity, see Glick (2009).
12. Recall Marx's sarcastic reproach of the Young Hegelians, '[T]he phantoms of their brains have got out of their hands ... Let us revolt against the rule of thoughts. Let us teach men ... to

exchange these imaginations for thought which correspond with the essence of man; says the second, to take up a critical attitude to them; says the third, to know them out of their heads; and – existing reality will collapse' (1970, p. 37).

13. For Rancière (2015) it is the fetishism of value rather than that of the commodity that is key. But note that he ultimately disavowed this reading (1976).
14. This point is vividly demonstrated in Appadurai's work. While he terms it a 'conceit,' Appadurai shows that commodities have 'social lives.'

Acknowledgements

An earlier version of this essay was presented at 'The Form Capitalism Gives to Our Lives' workshop at the Centre Marc Bloch, Berlin, September 2016, part of the 'Vulnerable & Dynamic Forms of Life' GDRI, an international, interdisciplinary research network supported by the CNRS. Thanks to Oz Frankel, Estelle Ferrarese, Emily Crandall, Elizabeth Stone, and the anonymous reviewers for *JCR* for their helpful comments. Additional thanks to Ariel Mekler for research assistance.

Disclosure statement

No potential conflict of interest was reported by the author.

References

Agamben, G. (2007). *Profanations*. Cambridge: MIT Press.

Althusser, L. (2006). Marx in his limits. In F. Matheron, & O. Corpet (Ed.), *Philosophy of the Encounter* (pp. 7–162). New York, NY: Verso.

Appadurai, A. (1986). *The social life of things: Commodities in cultural perspective*. New York, NY: Cambridge University Press.

Balibar, E. (2014). *The philosophy of Marx*. New York, NY: Verso.

Barad, K. (2003). Post humanist performativity: Toward an understanding of how matters comes to matter. *Signs: Journal of Women in Culture and Society, 28* (3), 801–831.

Baudrillard, J. (1981). *For a critique of the political economy of the sign*. (C. Levin, Trans.). Candor, NY: Telos Press.

Baumann, H. (1931). *Muret-Sanders Encyclopaedic English-German and German English Dictionary, Part II: German-English*. New York, NY: Frederick Ungar Publishing Company.

Bennett, J. (2001). *The Enchantment of Modern Life: Attachments, Crossings, and Ethics*. Princeton: Princeton University Press.

Bennett, J. (2004). The force of things: Steps toward an ecology of matter. *Political Theory, 32*(3), 347–372.

Bennett, J., (2010a). A vitalist stopover on the way to a new materialism. In D. Coole, & S. Frost (Ed.), *New materialisms: Ontology, agency, and politics* (pp. 47–69). Durham, NC: Duke University Press.

Bennett, J. (2010b). *Vibrant matter: A political ecology of things*. Durham, NC: Duke University Press.

de Brosse, C. (1760/1989). *Du Culte des Dieux Fétiches, ou Parallèle de l'ancienne Religion de l'Égypte avec la Religion actuelle de Nigritie*. Paris: Fayard.

Brown, B. (2001). Thing theory. *Critical Inquiry, 28*(1), 1–22.

Cheah, P. (2010). Non-dialectical materialism. In D. Coole, & S. Frost, *New materialisms: Ontology, agency, and politics* (pp. 70–91). Durham: Duke University Press.

Connolly, W. (2013). The new materialism and the fragility of things. *Millennium: Journal of International Studies, 41*(3), 399–412.

Coole, D., & Frost, S. (2010). *New materialisms: Ontology, agency, and politics*. Durham, NC: Duke University Press.

Delanda, M. (2006). *A new philosophy of society: Assemblage theory and social complexity*. London: Bloomsbury Academic.

Edwards, J. (2010). The materialism of historical materialism. In D. Coole, & S. Frost (Eds.), *New materialisms: Ontology, agency, and politics* (pp. 281–298). Durham, NC: Duke University Press.

Ferguson, K. (2013, March 28–30). Anarchist women printers: Old and new materialisms. *Western Political Science Association*. Hollywood, CA.

Foley, D. (1986). *Understanding capital: Marx's economic theory*. Cambridge: Harvard University Press.

Foucault, M. (1978). *The history of sexuality, Volume 1: An introduction*, New York, NY: Vintage.

Glick, E. (2009). *Materializing queer desire: Oscar Wilde to Andy Warhol*. Albany, NC: SUNY Press.

Hacker, P. M. S. 2013. Language, language-games, and forms of life. In J. P. Galvaz, & M. Gaffal (Eds.), *Forms of Life and Language Games* (17–36). Frankfurt: Ontos Verlag.

Heatherington, K. (2007). *Capitalism's eye: Cultural spaces of the commodity*. New York, NY: Routledge.

Hyman, S. E. (1962). *The tangled bank: Darwin, Marx, Frazer, and Freud as imaginative writers*. New York, NY: Atheneum.

Knappett, C., & Malafouris, L. (2008). *Material agency: Toward a non-anthropocentric approach*. New York, NY: Springer.

Latour, B. (1999). *Pandora's Hope: Essays on the reality of science studies*. Cambridge: Harvard University Press.

Latour, B. (2004). Why has critique run out of steam? From matters of fact to matters of concern. *Critical Inquiry, 30*(2), 225–248.

Latour, B. (2011). *The Prince and The Wolf: Latour and Harman at the LSE*. Washington, DC: Zero Books.

Lukacs, G. (1971). *History and class consciousness: Studies in Marxist dialectics*. Cambridge: MIT Press.

Marx, K. (1974). *Economic and philosophic manuscripts of 1844*. Moscow: Progress Publishers.

Marx, K. (1976). *Capital Volume 1: A critique of political economy*. New York, NY: Penguin.

Marx, K. (1981). *A contribution to the critique of political economy*. New York, NY: International Publishers.

Marx, K. (1993). *Grundrisse: Foundations of the critique of political economy*. New York, NY: Penguin.

Marx, K. (2000). *Capital Volume 3: A critique of political economy*. London: Electric Book Company. Available from: ProQuest Ebook Central. [28 October 2017].

Marx, K., & Engels, F. (1970). *The German ideology*. In C. J. Arthur (Ed.), New York, NY: International Publishers.

Marx, K., & Engels, F. (1996). *Collected works* (vol. 35). New York, NY: International Publishers.

Mulvey, L. (1996). *Fetishism and curiosity*. Bloomington, IN: Indiana University Press.

Rancière, J. (1976). How to use Lire le capital. *Economy and Society, 5*(3), 377–384.

Rancière, J. (2015). The concept of critique and the critique of political economy: From the 1884 manuscripts to capital. In L. Althusser (Ed.). *Reading capital* (pp. 73–170). London: Verso.

Rubin, I. I. (2008). *Essays on Marx's theory of value*. Delhi: Aakar Books.

Schmidt, Im., & Tanger, G. (1913). *Flügel-Schmidt-Tanger; A dictionary of the English and German languages for home and school*. (8th ed., vol. 2). Brunswick: G. Westerman.

Sypher, W. (1948). Aesthetic of revolution: The Marxian Melodrama. *The Kenyon Review, 10*(3), 431–444.

9 The whiteness of capital

Victoria Hattam

Everyday language anticipates capital mobility. Capital flows and liquid assets are invoked at every turn. But language deceives. There is nothing inherently mobile about capital: it is *made* mobile through an extensive network of structures and policies that enable capital to move. SWIFT codes, financial passporting, cross-border sweeping, and laser visas create conditions under which capital moves. As long as the mahouts of capital remain out of sight, capital mobility is naturalised and removed from political scrutiny. Following whiteness studies, I examine a wide array of facilitation policies that allow capital to move and in so doing uncover the linkages forged between race and class established through mobility and immobility (Alcoff, 2015; Baldwin, 1984; Du Bois, 1999; Harris, 1993; Morrison, 1981; Roediger, 1991). Once mobility policies that allow capital to cross international borders so readily are brought into view, new political possibilities also appear. Support for open borders expands once capital and labour mobility are considered simultaneously.

Capital, not labour, needs to be brought 'out of the shadows.'

Over the past four years, I have returned many times to the US-Mexico border, especially to the Rio Grande Valley.[1] Initially, I was drawn to the region because of the extensive border wall construction underway there. I wanted to bear witness to what was being built in my name. After several visits, the wall's allure began to fade. My attention shifted from the wall to the vibrant border economies along the Rio Grande. Cross border shoppers from Mexico filled the McAllen malls; long, long cargo trains passed through Laredo day and night; and ports of entry were being expanded and upgraded all along the valley. And I learned that 2000 managers cross daily from McAllen, Texas to Reynosa, Mexico. Focusing on border walls seemed insufficient – it seemed to miss where the action was taking place.

To understand how capital moves, I visited expediting zones, interviewed customs brokers and bridge directors, talked with journalists, academics, city officials, Fish and Wildlife employees, economic development corporations, border patrol agents, and political activists. In September of 2017, I attended the impressive Manufacturing and Logistics Conference in Laredo in where 350 people gathered at Texas A&M International to discuss cross border production and the impending revisions of NAFTA. I wanted to understand how capital moves.

Capital flows

Walls are always only a part of the bordering story. All borders *both* regulate *and* facilitate flows. As soon as questions of facilitation are bought into focus, an amazing array of institutions and policies come into view. Over the last half century, both the private and government sectors have introduced a number of policies to make capital mobile. In 1973, the private banking sector institutionalised SWIFT codes to facilitate the movement of money among banks; these codes are still actively used by individuals and institutions today (Scott & Zachariadis, 2012) BREXIT has drawn attention to 'cross border sweeping' and 'financial passporting' as important corporate policies facilitating trade (Golovtchenko, 2015). On the government front, NAFTA (1993), SENTRI (1995), F.A.S.T (2011), the Trade Facilitation and Trade Enforcement Acts (2012, 2013), the Cross Border Trade Enhancement Act 2016, and ACE (the automated trade environment act) all have been introduced to facilitate capital to flows. Although there is an excellent academic literature on border economies, for the most part, public debate has remained stubbornly focused on walls not trade (Lee & Wilson, 2014; Pipkin, 2012; Staudt, 1998).

Ports of entry

Capital mobility is materialised through ports of entry and customs brokerage firms. Ports of entry are especially interesting as they sit at the nexus of regulation and trade. How are these structures designed? By whom? What with money? To what ends?

Consider for a moment the International Bridge, in Phaar Texas. It is an impressive structure located within the small town of Phaar – population 76,538 (U.S. Census Bureau, n.d.). The ten lane bridge was opened in 1994 and is now one of the largest ports of entry along the Texas-Mexico border. Approximately 1500 trucks cross per day (540,151 trucks per year) (Phaar International Bridge, n.d.-a). To be sure, this is considerably lower volume than either Laredo or El Paso ports of entry, but what Phaar lacks in volume, it makes up for in sophistication. Some call Phaar 'the intelligent bridge' due to the 'state-of-the-art technology' in place; GAMA ray inspection and Free And Secure Trade (F.A.S.T) are in operation on both sides and Automated Commercial Environment (ACE) is on the way. The bridge authority boasts that Phaar has the fastest crossing times in the valley (Phaar International Bridge, n.d.-b). Bridge competition is intense; crossing times are critical.

Ports of entry ensure that capital moves. FAST Lanes, cooling and frozen goods inspection stations, and 'In bond' lots all allow capital not to stand in line. In bonding is key and as with most classification systems, the politics are carried in the details. To see where political openings might lie, we need to understand which goods enter in bond while others travel through regular lanes.

The criteria for entering in bond rests on whether the goods crossing the border are considered to be 'parts' or 'end products.' If a product is considered a part to be assembled, then under NAFTA, it can cross without paying duties by being transported 'in bond.' That is what the in bond lots are for; they allow goods that are in production to cross the border without duties. Think passenger transit lounges; in bond lots are the same for goods. So there is an enormous benefit in both time and price to being classified as a part to be assembled rather than a finished product. Consider, for example, windshield wipers and airbags. Both end up inside automobiles, but the path each takes across the border differs considerably. The wipers are considered products and taxed accordingly, while airbags enjoy smoother passage as parts and as such can cross the border via the in bond lots (Edinbarough, 2017).

Who decides what is a part and a whole? Through what processes? Based on what criteria? Answering these questions opens up critical aspects of bordering that have been obscured by the focus on walls. While U.S. trade policy is enacted through a myriad of national institutions, Customs and Border Protection (USCBP) is the *only* agency that can 'provide a legally binding advice or rulings on classification of imports.'[2] Fortunately, USCBP has created a searchable data base of customs rulings from 1989 to the present. The Customs Rulings Online Search System, or CROSS, includes original classification requests, facts of the cases, and holdings. Perhaps most important, for my purposes, each ruling lays out the reasoning behind each decision which is signed by the Director of Commercial Rulings Division. This is where production and trade intersect at a micro level.

Large corporations' ability to navigate ports of entry in ways that enhance capital flows was strengthened when President Obama signed the Cross Border Trade Enhancement Act into law on 16 December 2016. The statute introduced public-private partnerships for ports of entry via two important provisions: 'reimbursable services' and the 'donations acceptance program – CPB 559' (U.S. CBP, 2017b). By allowing private companies to foot the bill for infrastructural improvements and border patrol services, the statute broke with past practice in which ports of entry were exclusively state financed facilities.

Customs brokers and expediting companies

Structures alone do not make things move; customs brokers and expediting companies are essential to smooth and speedy cross-border flows. All of the larger towns along the Texas border from Brownsville to El Paso have many brokers at work. The town of Laredo, for example, which sits at the heart of the NAFTA corridor, has a population of 236,091 and is home to 225 customs brokerage firms. This is equivalent to one expediting company for every 1049 people and since each of these firms has several employees, the ratio of brokers to residents is even lower than these numbers indicate (U.S. CBP, 2017b). Moreover, these figures most likely undercount the number of brokers, as they do not include the customs brokerage firms registered across the border in Nuevo Laredo (U.S. CBP, 2017a). Facilitating border crossing of goods is a vibrant business.

Unlike the border walls, the expediting zones are not telegenic. They are isolated, desolate places. Perhaps facilitation policies receive so little media attention because these locations are visually unappealing. Do not be distracted; this is where the political action is. These are the people and companies that make capital flow. Note the company logos – no borderlines here! Where maps appear, they show contiguous territories annotated with arrows and swirls. Movement is what these companies are selling (Figure 1).

Considering regulation and facilitation together changes the politics of bordering. Popular cries to 'secure the border' take on a different significance if security is understood as applying to *both* capital and labour.

Figure 1. Lopezadri Freight Forwarding, Laredo, Texas. 6 March, 2016. Photograph by Hattam.

Politics

How might attending to facilitation change border politics? I see three political implications from this analysis presented here. First, riveting as border wall photographs are, it is a mistake to make walls the central focus of border politics. The danger lies in the ways in which walls divert attention from the many policies that allow capital to move. Forget the wall – it is a distraction. Focus instead on capital flows. Expediting zones, trucking lots, and FAST lanes – those are the sites in need of politicization (Figure 2).

Second, attending to policies that facilitate capital flows places questions of equality front and centre. One can imagine open or closed border regimes that, despite their differences on cross-border mobility, might nevertheless treat labour and capital equally. A closed border regime might foster separate economic ecologies with little interaction between the two. In this instance, both labour and capital might have limited abilities to cross. Similarly, an open border regime might allow both capital and labour to move equally. Indeed, this was the premise of the Schengen Agreement. The equality principle thus need not specify a preference for open or closed; rather the issue is whether mobility is offered to labour and capital in roughly equal increments. Both might be allowed to move, or both might be restricted.

Currently, the United States explicitly eschews equal treatment of labour and capital at the border; very different mobility policies apply to the crossings of differently positioned goods and services. Put simply, labour is regulated and capital facilitated. As border policies now stand, there is little need for capital to support open borders as they have it both ways. They can call for border security, without ever having to contend with restricted access to

Figure 2. Trucking depot, McAllen, Texas. February 7, 2017. Photograph by Hattam.

border crossing. Capital is not made to stand in line. If trucks and trains loaded with goods had to wait for hours and hours at the ports of entry, business executives might think twice about 'securing the border.' Currently, only labour is made to stand in line while capital is waved on through.

The destructive aspects of U.S. border politics lie in the asymmetrical mobility rights afforded labour and capital. The policies facilitating the movement of capital continue to fly under the radar. Ignoring the advantages afforded US manufacturing and trade undercuts the formation of a broad based open borders coalition. Pushing for more equitable mobility conditions might open up new political possibilities; there are real fissures within business communities and within the Republican Party that might be pushed open. Doing so, might allow new coalitions to emerge.

Notes

1. This paper grows out of research conducted by the Multiple Mobilities Working Group at the New School: https://www.multiplemobilities.org/. I am indebted to all of the participants and thank them for their friendship and intellectual vitality. I also appreciate support from the Zolberg Institute for our collaborative projects.
2. For the singular role of U.S. Customs and Border Protection and customs rulings, see the United States International Trade Commission, 'Official Harmonized Tariff Schedule 2017,' p. 1. https://www.usitc.gov/tata/hts/index.htm.

Disclosure statement

No potential conflict of interest was reported by the author.

References

Alcoff, L. (2015). *The future of whiteness*. New York, NY: Polity.

Baldwin, J. (1984). On being white … and other lies. *Essence, 14*(12), 90–92.

Du Bois, W. E. B. (1999). *Darkwater: Voices from within the Veil*. Mineola, NY: Dover Publications.

Edinbarough, Immanuel. (2017). Rapid response manufacturing center. Interview at UT-RGV Brownsville campus. February 3.

Golovtchenko, V. (2015). HSBC to launch renminbi cross-border sweeping with Germany. *Finance Magnates*. Retrieved February 27, 2018, from https://www.financemagnates.com/forex/analysis/hsbc-launch-renminbi-cross-border-sweeping-germany/

Harris, C. I. (1993). Whiteness as property. *Harvard Law Review, 106*(8), 1707–1791.

Lee, E., & Wilson, C. (2014). *The U.S.-Mexico border economy in transition*. Washington, DC: Woodrow Wilson International Center for Scholars. Retrieved February 27, 2018, from https://www.wilsoncenter.org/publication/the-us-mexico-border-economy-transition

Morrison, T. (1981). Unspeakable things unspoken: The Afro-American presence in American literature. *Michigan Quarterly Review, 28*(1), 1–34.

Phaar International Bridge. (n.d.-a). *About us*. Retrieved February 27, 2018, from http://bridge.pharr-tx.gov/x-about/

Phaar International Bridge. (n.d.-b). *Truck crossing comparison*. Retrieved February 27, 2018, from http://bridge.pharr-tx.gov/crossings-revenues/total-crossings-comparison/truck-crossing-comparison

Pipkin, S. D. (2012). *Repertoires of development in economic divergence on the U.S. – Mexico border*. PhD thesis, Massachusetts Institute of Technology.

Roediger, D. R. (1991). *The wages of whiteness: Race and the making of the American working class*. New York, NY: Verso.

Scott, S. V., & Zachariadis, M. (2012). Origins and development of SWIFT, 1973–2009. *Business History, 54*(3), 462–482.

Staudt, K., (1998). *Free trade: Informal economies at the U.S.-Mexico border*. Philadelphia, PA: Temple University Press.

U.S. CBP. (2017a). *Brokers*. Retrieved February 27, from https://apps.cbp.gov/brokers/index.asp?portCode=23042018

U.S. CBP. (2017b). *Donations acceptance program – Announcements*. Retrieved February 27, 2018, from https://www.cbp.gov/border-security/ports-entry/resource-opt-strategy/public-private-partnerships/donation-acceptance-program

U.S. Census Bureau. (n.d.). *QuickFacts: Pharr city, Texas, The United States Census Bureau*. Retrieved February 27, 2018, from https://www.census.gov/quickfacts/fact/table/pharrcitytexas/PST045216

10 Beyond the barricades

Class interests and actually existing black life

Cedric G. Johnson

In his 1962 essay 'Revolutionary Nationalism and the Afro-American,' Harold Cruse quipped, 'American Marxists cannot "see" the Negro at all, unless he is storming the barricades, either in the present or in history' (Cruse, 1968). An ex-communist, Cruse took issue with his former comrades who only focused on resistance that comported with socialist sensibilities. Their selective history produced a view of the black population as 'a people without classes or differing class interests.' And yet, Cruse ultimately undermines his sharpest insights regarding the complex internal political life of black communities, insisting that like the wage laborer and sharecropper, who are discriminated against and exploited, the 'educated, professional and intellectual classes suffer a similar fate.' From this common Jim Crow predicament, Cruse urges the Negro bourgeoisie to operate as a national bourgeoisie who will undertake the tasks of building group economic and political autonomy. The myth of an organic black constituency has gained renewed legitimacy as thousands have returned to the barricades to protest police violence. Sadly, some contemporary leftists can only 'see the Negro' when he appears in viral videos of police wilding, or the demonstrations that follow. In contrast, this essay calls for a critical analysis of actually-existing black life, one that ventures beyond the barricades to account for the historically-contingent political and material interests that animate black politics and connect the situated-class experiences of blacks to those of all others living under capitalism.

The slogan, 'Black Lives Matter,' crafted by three queer feminist activists after the vigilante killing of unarmed teen Trayvon Martin, reasserts a common black plight and demands an end to racist violence. The phrase challenged the discourse of post-racialism that accompanied Barack Obama's ascent to the presidency and his approach to governing, which was defined by a willingness to confine racial grievance to the past and a penchant for underclass moralizing. In the wake of the election of Donald J. Trump, debates have sharpened between the poles of nativist, pro-policing reaction and liberal anti-racism, and race and racism have ossified as the central categories for discussing American inequality. The vicissitudes of the moment have encouraged an accounting of black life that fails to learn from the more than half century of black political development and meaningful progress that has taken place since Cruse's formative criticisms of the Left's inability to see black life as possessing multiple classes and historical interests. Black Lives Matter, and kindred analytic frames like the New

Jim Crow possess a certain utility as political slogans, but falter as social analysis because they approach the problems of policing and prisons as being felt universally by the black population, and some believe, with little impact on others, especially whites (Alexander, 2010). A closer examination of the historical evolution of the carceral state finds its roots, not in Jim Crow, but in the class recomposition and nascent social conflicts of the postwar consumer society.

Policing as we know it took shape during the Cold War as a means of securing the property rights of capital *and* the new suburban middle class, and simultaneously as a means of managing surplus population, those made redundant by labor-saving technology. The view that mass incarceration and hyperpolicing are part of a longer unbroken thread stretching back to the antebellum slave-catching patrols has been widely circulated in popular culture. That narrative, however, does not square with historical fact, and mystifies the actual forces responsible for the exponential expansion of US prison populations in the waning decades of the twentieth century. In 1940, during a period of entrenched Jim Crow segregation, the vast majority of prisoners in America's state and federal institutions, some 73 percent, were white (Calahan & Parsons, 1986). The proportion of white inmates would decline gradually, as suburbanization, vigorous economic growth, massive infrastructure improvements and heavy investment in public schools and higher education all combined to transform millions of Americans into nominal property-holders and members of the new consumer middle class (Cohen, 2004).

Blacks were largely excluded from the post-war prosperity, due to formal Jim Crow strictures and a commercial Keynesian context that treated private actors, developers, realtors and homeowners as sovereign, enabling all manner of discrimination at the local level. Rather than viewing the black condition as exceptional and race as the singular determinant of black life, a closer examination of black experiences of the postwar urban transformation throws into relief different subject positions and often conflicting interests. We see blacks leaving hazardous slum tenements for newly constructed public housing. Well-established black neighborhoods and commercial corridors are bulldozed to clear the ground for highway construction and urban renewal. Angry crowds face down blue-collar black families as they attempt to purchase homes in white neighborhoods. Black professionals and artists live next door and in relative harmony with whites in the more urbane reaches of society. We see black landlords who behave like white landlords, and black developers posing for photos with gilded shovels in hand as they break ground on exclusive subdivisions for professionals.

The postwar civil rights movement sought the restoration of black citizenship in the South, but also access to the jobs and prosperity denied by Jim Crow (Jones, 2013). Some of the most pitched battles for desegregation unfolded in consumption and leisure spaces—lunch counters, pharmacies, department stores, public pools and beaches, and concert halls. Of course, black critics of the southern desegregation campaigns grew increasingly skeptical of the capacity of civil rights reforms to create meaningful progress, and by the middle sixties, demands for black political autonomy and real self-determination literally spread like wild fire across America's cities. The most radical black power voices articulated a nascent critique of the prison system, one that made clear the class relations shaping the black population and American society writ large.

Civil rights reforms created the context for a long and uneven process of black integration into the consumer society, but the same capitalist dynamics that made all manner of goods and lifestyles available to millions of Americans also produced chronic unemployment for the black urban poor through corporate restructuring and more capital-intensive production, strategies adopted in response to growing worker power. We get a sense of the emergent nexus of unemployment and incarceration in the writings of George Jackson, the co-founder of the Black Guerilla Family who was killed in 1971 during an attempted escape from San Quentin prison. 'This is my eleventh year of being shoveled into every major prison in the most populous state in the nation—and the largest prison system in the world,' Jackson wrote, 'at each institution I've been in, 30 to sometimes 40 percent of those held are black, and every one of the many thousands I've encountered was from the working or lumpen-proletariat class.' (Jackson, 1996) So while Jackson is clear that blacks are overrepresented, he insists that there is an underlying unity, the vast majority of the prison population is drawn from the most dispossessed, sub-proletariat. The Black Panther Party and related organizations like the Young Lords and the Young Patriots, developed strategies for challenging police abuse, from the early armed police-monitoring patrols undertaken in Oakland, to demands for greater public oversight and accountability in Chicago. These efforts were heroic, but were ultimately inadequate to the enormity of the task at hand, which required not merely the mobilization of the ghetto poor, but the transformation of a society where millions had come to see the interests of capital as their own, and now accepted the role of domestic policing and imperial wars in maintaining the prosperity they enjoyed. In this Cold War context of middle-class complicity, the Panthers and other urban radical-left organizations were isolated and repressed by state and federal police agencies.

In the decades following the mass urban rebellions of the sixties, race emerged as the dominant symbolic language of American inequality. If 'white' became a synonym for middle class, suburban, law-abiding and virtuous, property-owning, hardworking, and self-governing, then 'black' came to function as a euphemism for poor, urban, criminal and dysfunctional, dispossessed, lazy, and dependent. Contemporary anti-racist discourse contests these pejorative connotations of blackness, but obscure the actual historical interests that propelled the expansion of more aggressive modes of policing from Richard Nixon's initial declaration of the War on Drugs to the militarized policing that lay at the heart of urban revanchism, the literal taking back of the city by real-estate developers and corporations beginning in the late eighties. The popular claim that racism is the central motive force of the prison build-up forgets the complex history of over a half-century of black urban governance.

Black power as political incorporation became a reality, with most major American cities electing black mayors and often majority-black city councils. These black-led cities, however would inherit a number of well-known constraints on their capacity to govern, such as declining tax bases, population loss, capital flight, declining federal investment, archaic infrastructure and worsening social conditions (Reed, 1999). Within this difficult social context, civic leaders made even more difficult policy choices, with some blacks supporting anti-crime measures because of idiosyncratic political beliefs, and others because of their specific constituent interests, e.g. as homeowners, victims' families, etc., just like similarly-situated whites.

James Forman, Jr.'s *Locking Up Our Own* offers a highly textured account of how and why some residents, politicians and activists in Washington, D.C. supported a politics of incarceration during an era of black political control (Forman, 2017). In his study, we find divergent and historically discrete motives for black support of various criminal justice policies. Black civil rights activists in Atlanta during the 1940s and the District of Columbia in the 1960s demanded the hiring of more black officers as a remedy to police brutality. During the seventies, black nationalists opposed marijuana legalization in the District because they viewed it as a 'gateway' drug to more dangerous addictions. Some black judges insisted on harsh punishment for black violent offenders out of a moral obligation to black victims, who for too long were denied adequate police protection or court justice under Jim Crow. These decisions were made with an eye towards what might be done to reduce addiction, theft and violence within a context of limited choices. This history contradicts activist sloganeering and analyses that portray the problems of policing and mass incarceration in stark black and white terms, and instead, he gives a more nuanced historical appreciation of why certain constituencies supported policies that would eventually have a disastrous effect on black incarceration rates. Forman's work presents us with a political paradox that remains instructive in this era of resurgent liberal identity politics, that is, the fact of black political control did not protect black District residents from the escalating problems of crime and policing. Rather, within the all-black context of the District, specific constituencies combined to produce measures that had unintended consequences, efforts to protect victims and reduce drug crime and violence contributed to mass incarceration.

Racial affinity and ascriptive status should not be mistaken for political constituency, and an understanding of the different ways black life is constituted by capitalist class relations will be crucial to any success that police-reform forces might achieve going forward. In cities like Baltimore and Chicago, which possess racially integrated police forces and city administrations, massive anti-policing protests have been defused and placated through legal prosecution of police, suspensions and firings. Street demonstrations have also been met with the mobilization of more centrist black political elements, who have called for modest technical reforms to correct police abuse, such as body cameras, as well as advancing private-charitable projects and volunteer mentoring as solutions to poverty (Johnson, 2016). In large, complex urban areas, where black power has been institutionalized and entrenched, analyses that ignore the actually-existing class relations and interests shaping mass incarceration and the political arena will do little to advance the kind of substantive reforms touted by the most progressive elements of anti-policing protests.

Disclosure statement

No potential conflict of interest was reported by the author.

References

Alexander, M. (2010). *The new Jim Crow: Mass incarceration in the age of colorblindness*. New York, NY: New Press.

Calahan, M., & Parsons, L. (1986). *Historical corrections statistics in the United States, 1850–1984*. Rockville, MD: Westat, Inc. and U.S. Department of Justice/Bureau of Justice Statistics.

Cohen, L. (2004). *A consumer's republic: The politics of mass consumption in postwar America*. New York, NY: Vintage.

Cruse, H. (1968). *Rebellion or revolution?*. New York, NY: William Morrow.

Forman, J., Jr. (2017). *Locking up our own: Crime and punishment in Black America*. New York, NY: Farrar, Straus and Giroux.

Jackson, G. (1996). *Blood in my eye*. Baltimore, MD: Black Classics.

Johnson, C. (2016). Afterword: Baltimore, the policing crisis and the end of the Obama era. In J. DeFilippis, (Ed.), *Urban policy in the time of Obama* (pp. 302–321). Minneapolis, MN: University of Minnesota Press.

Jones, W. (2013). *The march on Washington: Jobs, freedom and the forgotten history of civil rights*. New York, NY: W.W. Norton.

Reed, A. (1999). *Stirrings in the jug: Black politics in the postsegregation era*. Minneapolis, MN: University of Minnesota Press.

11 The capitalist metabolism

An unachieved subsumption of life under the value-form

Timothée Haug

ABSTRACT
This article views capitalism not only as a mode of production, but also as a mediation of the reproduction of life (human and non-human), following the concept of 'social metabolism' that Marx employs to analyze the interaction between the individuals composing a society and their natural environment. Insofar as the 'value-form' is the distinctive social relation of capitalism, it appears necessary to ask whether the metabolic process of reproduction can be fully subsumed under this form. Marx takes for granted the idea that the reproduction of labor-power consists only in the consumption of commodities resulting from abstract labor, thus omitting the appropriation of unpaid domestic work, mostly performed by women. Feminist criticism clarifies how capitalism always depends on some reproductive work being appropriated for the accumulation of surplus-value without being integrated in the value-form. Following Jason W. Moore, I attempt to indicate that the same logic is at work for the reproduction of non-human life under the capitalist value-form, thus contradicting the sustainable reproduction of its own natural conditions. These two limitations of the capitalist subsumption of life open a new space for an expanded critique of capitalism, which goes beyond the exploitation of waged work by reflecting upon the concerns of feminist and ecological struggles.

The development of social movements after the 1960s enabled a broader understanding of the capitalist mode of production while extending the scope of its critique to the exploitation of unpaid domestic work and the destructive appropriation of natural resources (Fraser, 2014). Engaged in the 'Wages for Housework' campaign, feminists from both Italy and the USA underlined women's specific domination in the household, whose unpaid work contributes to lowering working wages (Federici, 1975; James & Dalla Costa, 1972). Simultaneously, ecological protests denounced the careless exploitation of ecosystems providing the raw materials and energies necessary for the capitalist accumulation (Bookchin, 1971). These two struggles met in an ecofeminist[1] movement, which emerged during the classes Ynestra King gave at the Institute of Social Ecology in Vermont. It found its first political expression through the 'Women's Pentagon Action' in 1980, when thousands of women encircled the Pentagon to protest the destructive impact the nuclear industry has on both human and non-human life (Merchant, 2005, pp. 194–195). Although a 'socialist' school of ecofeminism attempts to break away from its more 'cultural' trend – which tends to presuppose the nature-relatedness of women without criticizing the patriarchal background of this association – it still remains necessary to propose a non-essentialist account of the connection between women's emancipation and the defense of the environment. In *Rethinking Ecofeminist Politics*, Janet Biehl denounces the metaphorical rhetoric underlying the ecofeminist equation and takes a stand for an ecosocialist critique of capitalism.[2] However, instead of considering feminist and ecological issues as two independent questions, I would like to follow the insights of later ecofeminist writers (Mellor, 1997; Mies, 2014; Salleh, 1997) in order to engage a critical confrontation with Marxist theory. This might enable us to locate the structural connection between the capitalist domination of 'women' and 'nature'.

In order to analyze this twofold dynamic, it appears useful to open up the classical Marxist definition of capitalism as a 'mode of production' and attempt to consider it also as a 'form of life'. The first theoretical scheme, which understands each society according to the organization of its production, distinguishes within it the technical interaction with nature – productive forces – and the normative interactions between individuals composing this society – relations of production. Against such a divide between socialized human life and external nature, it appears necessary to underline their complex interaction by studying the integration of life processes within social relations. Life processes encompass both the reproduction of human life and the reproduction of non-human life in ecosystems. Both of them represent, as labor force and natural resources, two conditions of the capitalist production of goods and accumulation of value. As shown by the *Neue Marx-Lektüre* (Backhaus, 2011) and the so-called Value-Form theory (Arthur, 2004), 'value' is the specific capitalist form, which integrates the relations of exchange and production in the social totality. Following its own logic, capitalism tends to subsume life itself – human and non-human – under this form, by defining it as a virtual commodity and the product of abstract labor. In the real world, however, this economical system still depends on two main 'externalities' to reproduce itself: the unpaid reproductive work performed mostly by women outside of the market and the appropriation of free natural resources. In order to articulate feminist struggles over domestic work and ecological concerns about the destruction of ecosystems, it is necessary to question the limits of capitalist forms of life. This means asking how far the reproduction of life can be subsumed under the value-form.

The capitalist form of life as social metabolism

What does it mean to analyze a social organization, such as capitalism, as a 'form of life'? First and foremost, such a definition has to depart from a naturalist account of human life, identifying its form with an ahistorical essence. This reductionism is already overcome by Marx and Engels' shift carried out in the *German Ideology* from a naturalist concept of 'mode of life' (*Lebensweise*) to the sociological category of 'mode of production' (*Produktionsweise*) (Marx & Engels, 1975, p. 58). However, the methodological scheme of the 'mode of production' entails a new kind of dualism between the so-called productive forces and relations of production, *i.e.* the technical bonds between Nature and Society on the one hand and the human interactions within society on the other hand. To avoid such a split, the concept of 'form of life' should also be distinguished from a dualist framework separating social forms of interactions and a biological basis supposedly remaining outside of social relations.

From this perspective, it will be helpful to examine to the concept of 'metabolism' (*Stoffwechsel*) that Marx employs to describe both the interaction of society as a whole to nature and the relation of the living individual to its environment (Foster, 2000; Marx, 1996; Salleh, 1997). In its scientific meaning, the term 'metabolism' defines the connection of an organism to its environment as a permanent exchange of material components which aims at maintaining a formal identity. In this sense, it is precisely the essential characteristic of life to have a form, to be a form, while its material substratum continuously changes. For example, the vegetal growth is based on the combination of an assimilation of minerals lying in the ground and a photosynthetic process, while the animal metabolism requires both the absorption of organic substances through digestion and oxygen through respiration. In the introduction of the *Grundrisse*, Marx implicitly refers to this organic process when he defines the concept of 'production' laying the basis of his economical inquiry. For every kind of organism, whether vegetal, animal or human, the production of the living form is *immediately* equal to the consumption of elements extracted from the environment:

> Consumption is also immediately production, just as in nature the consumption of the elements and chemical substances is the production of the plant. It is clear that in taking in food, for example, which is a form of consumption, the human being produces his own body. But this is also true of every kind of consumption which in one way or another produces human beings in some particular aspect. Consumptive production. (Marx, 1973, pp. 90–91)

If this 'consumptive production' remains the basis of human metabolism, the anthropological difference comes precisely from the disjunction of production and consumption through the mediation of work. In this case, the consumptive production of an individual's life is no longer realized through a direct appropriation of given things found in the environment but presupposes the transformation of those things in objects of consumption. As a process of objectification, production is never the result of isolated individual activity, but proceeds from cooperation and division of labor. To that extent, the human 'life form' always requires a *social* 'form of life',[3] organizing production and articulating it to consumption. To put it simply, the biological metabolism of human life is always mediated by a social form of production and distribution through a process that Marx names 'social metabolism' in his late work (1998, p. 799).[4] The mediation of the biological metabolism by the social metabolism is twofold: on one side it depends on a technical development of the production and on the other side, it depends on an economical organization of the production. In order to analyze a social form as a mode of production but also *as well* as a form of life, I will attempt to offer a critical reinterpretation of the Marxist concept of metabolism. With such a perspective in mind, metabolism should be understood as describing the reproduction, not only of society as a whole, but also of the individuals composing this totality.[5]

Life in the web of value

The critical study of capitalism as a specific configuration of the reproduction of life within society is carried out by Marx in the two first chapters of the first book of *Capital*. Here he proceeds from the definition of the commodity to the analysis of the buying and selling of labor-power.

Simply put, the category of commodity designates the kind of things that are produced in capitalist society so as to be exchanged on the market. To that extent, the commodity does not only possess a use-value, which defines its ability to satisfy a concrete need, but also an exchange-value, which relates to its potentiality to be exchanged with qualitatively different commodities. Such an exchange can only function if there is a common quantitative feature shared by all commodities which, according to classical political economy, is the duration of labor expended in their production. Marx underlines that the 'value-form' of the commodity defines the complex interaction between its exchange on the market and the labor from which it proceeds, so that the average amount of 'abstract labor' necessary for its production is set by competition operating throughout the market.[6]

In the chapter dedicated to 'The Buying and Selling of Labour Power', Marx demonstrates that this value-form does not only determine the objects produced in capitalism, but also the living individuality of the workers (1996, pp. 177–186). Indeed, the capitalist entrepreneur acquires raw materials and machines, but also pays wages in exchange for the labor-power of his employees. How, then, is the value of labor to be defined, if labor itself is the measure of value? This is the critical knot at the core of the capitalist mode of production. Actually, what is bought by the capitalist is not the labor itself but the laborer's capacity to work, which Marx names labor-power. 'By labour power or capacity for labour is to be understood the aggregate of those physical and mental capabilities existing in a human being, which he exercises whenever he produces a use-value of any description' (1996, p. 177). In order to be bought and sold on the labor market, this labor-power has to be considered as a commodity. This means that the production and the reproduction of the worker's organic body and all its intellectual capacities can be assessed as the result of a given amount of previous labor. Such an extension of the objective form of the commodity to the subjective capacity of work itself represents the very definition of the capitalist form of life. Of course, this does not mean that the entire life of an individual is put on sale, as in the case of slavery. In the logic of the value-form, the reproduction of the worker's living individuality is *supposed* to be fully mediated by the consumption of commodities already produced by abstract labor.

But what does such a reproduction mean? As Marx puts it, it requires a series of objects necessary to satisfy the worker's fundamental needs[7]: food, clothes, housing, furniture, etc., and a series of services such as education and health-care. However, the every-day 'maintenance' of the actual workers is not sufficient to fulfill the labor market's requirements, because each worker is a living and hence a finite being:

> The owner of labour power is mortal. If then his appearance in the market is to be continuous, and the conversion of money into capital assumes this, the seller of labour power must perpetuate himself, "in the way that every living individual perpetuates himself by procreation". The labour power withdrawn from the market by wear and tear and death, must be continually replaced by, at the very least, an equal amount of fresh labour-power. Hence the sum of the means of subsistence necessary for the production of labour power must include the means necessary for the labourer's substitutes, *i.e.*, his children, in order that this race of peculiar commodity-owners may perpetuate its appearance in the market. (1996, pp. 181–182)

Quoting the economist William Petty, Marx not only depicts the integration of the life process in the market as an ontogenetic reproduction – the subsistence of the single individual through her own organic metabolism, but also as a phylogenetic reproduction – the perpetuation of the working class over generations. Consequently, the whole metabolic cycle is reduced to a simple consumption of commodities, produced through the cash-nexus of the market, producing living beings ready to be employed.

In Marx's systematic understanding of capitalism, abstract labor time expended in the form of waged work is the very principle on which the whole social structure is based. Its own subject, the labor-power, is supposed to be wholly reproduced in the realm of the market as the objectified result of labor condensed in the form of commodities. Referring to Marx's own concepts, we could say that an achieved capitalism would carry out real subsumption, not only to the production process but also of the reproduction process of life, under the value-form. However, the new light thrown by the feminist critique of double exploitation in waged work *as well as* in domestic activities, emphasizes the limits of this subsumption.

The split form of human life under capitalism

Together with the 1970s 'Wages for housework' campaigns, second-wave feminists criticized the reductionist definition of 'reproduction' presupposed in Marx's analysis of the renewal of the labor-force as a simple consumption of commodities (James & Dalla Costa, 1972; Federici, 1975). Indeed, such a definition misses the specificity of living metabolism by comparing it with a mechanical process:

> But the man, like the machine, will wear out, and must be replaced by another man. Beside the necessaries required for his own maintenance, he wants another amount of necessaries to bring up a certain quota of children that are to replace him on the labour market and to perpetuate the race of labourers. (Marx, 1985, p. 129)

This metaphorical identification of the reproduction of labor force with the maintenance and replacement of other means of production is highly delusive, since it hampers a proper understanding of the specific tasks performed outside of waged work to sustain and renew life, such as cooking, washing, cleaning, raising and educating children, taking care of the elderly, etc. After their first attempt to extend the Marxist concept of work so as to include those activities performed mostly by women (Benston, 1980), second-wave feminists split around the so-called 'domestic labor debate'. Some materialist feminists abandoned the Marxist framework to analyze the specificity of a patriarchal domination distinct from the capitalist mode of production .[8] Here, I will attempt to take a stand for a renewed feminist reading of Marx, which tries to understand the complex interaction between those two kinds of domination (Barrett, 2014). Instead of simply rejecting the Marxist definition of value, I propose to follow a feminist reinterpretation of the Marxist value-form theory (Scholz, 2011), characterizing unpaid reproductive work as the result of an unachieved integration of the reproduction of human life into the market.

As opposed to constant capital, which can be reproduced through the buying of commodities within the market, the reproduction of labor-power takes place outside of this realm and depends on unpaid domestic activities. This distinction is not only true for the phylogenetic reproduction of the successive generations of workers, which relies on the bearing and breeding of children, but also for the ontogenetic reproduction of the single worker, which cannot simply be summed up to the purchase of commodities. The use-value of a commodity is only an abstract economic concept, which does not describe the series of domestic tasks required to fulfill the metabolic process. This process appears clearly in the transformation of products purchased on the market, such as food, into consumption goods but is also true of other useful objects such as clothes, furniture, etc. Even if they are sold as ready-for-use goods, they have to be washed, cleaned, or repaired (Scholz, 2011, p. 25).

One could however object that far from being absolute, the autonomy of reproduction from the market is only historically relative. Indeed, the gap separating commodity production within the market and the reproduction process might be overcome by a progress in the technological means of production and reproduction. The increase of consumption triggered by the Fordist mode of production since the 1920s resulted in such a tendency. The second half of the century witnessed the selling of processed food and disposable goods, the progressive mechanization of housework enabled by new appliances, and the development of the service industry. On the one hand, this permitted a larger integration of the ontogenetic reproduction of the individual within the capitalist form of life (Lukács, 2011, pp. 455–457). On the other hand, the rapid development of assisted reproductive techniques since the 1970s entailed the emergence of a capitalist 'mode of reproduction' (Thompson, 2005, p. 248). These new technological possibilities enabled the commodification of phylogenetic reproduction itself, as exemplified by the development of a market of surrogate pregnancy (Dickenson, 2008).

However, the integration of the biological metabolism within the capitalist form (the social metabolism) cannot be reduced to a technological change. Even if new technologies open new possibilities for the commodification of life, by producing what was previously only re-produced, these are only possibilities which still have to be integrated in the economic value-form in order to by fully commodified. A closer look at the economical function of *unpaid* reproductive activities, as a factor of surplus-value extraction, indicates that the subsumption of the reproduction process under the value-form remains limited for economic reasons. Here, it is important to remember that the value of labor-power (as wage) is determined by the amount of commodities required to sustain the worker's life and to spawn new workers. An increase in the commodification of reproduction consequently implies a rising value of the labor-power and a decrease in the profit share, since all the costs of the unpaid work of women are internalized in the labor market. It is true that a large increase in productivity can partly offset these costs by reducing the basic price of commodities, and consequently the value of labor-power. However, this tendency remains limited to the market of consumption goods. Indeed, the raise of productivity is very limited for care-work, including child bearing and breeding, since these activities are not time-compressible (Haug, 1996). Although this care-work can be performed outside of the domestic sphere and childbearing can be sold and bought through surrogate pregnancy, their commodification always entails a rise in the value of labor-power, which represents extra costs for the employers. This means that the value-form cannot subsume the totality of the life process and its reproduction without undermining the capitalist accumulation of surplus-value. Contrary to Marx's first assumption, capitalist accumulation necessarily depends on unpaid reproductive work.

Against any systematic account of capitalism as an economic form encompassing the whole metabolic process, in its ontogenetic and phylogenetic dimensions, one should take into account the obverse side of reproduction that cannot be absorbed by the commodity system. The value-form, which characterizes the capitalist mode of production, can only determine the 'waged' form of life insofar as it constantly excludes a series of unwaged activities out of its realm. According to the value-separation (*Wert-Abspaltung*) theory developed by Roswitha Scholz, this split is inherent to the abstraction of value, which dialectically depends on its opposite: the unpaid and invisible reproductive activities. Rather than a pre-capitalist realm, which is *not yet* integrated in the market, the domestic area represents an essential moment of this social mode of production, and implies a specific logic of domination distinct from the waged form of labor, *i.e.* patriarchy. By acknowledging such limitation one does not reject Marx's analysis of waged work as a distinctive capitalist form of life. As demonstrated by Scholz, waged work has to be considered as the one visible and acknowledged side of a split form of life. Meanwhile the other side remains excluded by the logic of valuation implemented under capitalism (Scholz, 2011, p. 24). This 'separated' area (*das Abgespaltene*), as she calls it, encompasses all the activities that remain necessary to connect and mediate the purchase of commodities and the metabolic process of reproduction, *e.g.* the preparation and repairs of commodities for consumption, the maintenance of the household and the bearing and breeding of children. As a split form of life, capitalism is characterized by the non-valuation of this realm excluded from waged work, made to be invisible and determined according to gender. It entails an *unachieved* integration of the life process in the realm of value production. This limitation is however not to be understood as a relative boundary to be overcome by any technological development, but rather as a fundamental divide based on the value-form specific to capitalism.

Capitalism and the expanded reproduction of life.

Marx's short-sightedness with regards to the reproductive work required to complete the human metabolism outside of the market, reflects the very logic of value on which capitalism is based. The value-form is not only 'abstract' in the sense that it reduces the qualitative diversity of things to the same quantitative measure, but also in the sense that it remains blind to the specificity of the biological processes on which economic production depends. Far from being a sheer mistake without reality, such an abstraction corresponds to existing dynamics of exclusion and devaluation of 'externalities.' To overcome the simple metaphoric association between the domination of women and the appropriation of nature, presupposed by the ecofeminist rhetoric, I would like to delineate a structural analogy between both sides of the reproduction of life. Both human and non-human life are subjected to the value-form without being wholly integrated in it.

Whilst studying the cycle of the capitalist production and its relation to external 'nature' in his *Manuscripts of 1857–1858* (*Grundrisse*), Marx first adopts a perspective very similar to his analysis of the reproduction of labor-power. From the consideration [*Betrachtung*] of a developed capitalist society, non-human nature is *supposedly* integrated in the value-form, by being the product of abstract labor. As opposed to hunter-gather or feudal societies confronted to an 'external' nature, the capitalist mode of production concretely (re)produces the natural environment from within, for example through industrial forestry or capitalized farming. In this work, Marx seems to identify this production of nature with the achieved subsumption of non-human life's reproduction under the value-form. In a footnote to the manuscript, dealing with the global process of reproduction, he still resorts to Hegelian rhetoric so as to describe capital as an all-encompassing totality, internalizing all kind of externalities, including waste: 'Finally, products entering into final consumption in turn come out of consumption as raw materials for production, fertilizer in the process of nature etc., paper out of rags etc.' (Marx, 1973, p. 717). In his seminal book of 1984, the radical geographer Neil Smith deepens Marx's insight through the thesis of a 'production of nature' in industrial capitalism, here understood as the mediation of concrete natural processes by exchange-value (Smith, 1990). But contrary to Marx, Smith emphasizes the ecological destruction resulting from the capitalist production of nature, a mastery spiraling out of control and generating massive amounts of waste unable to be integrated by the value-form.

However, Marx himself acknowledged this specific capitalist destruction of nature, when he later reworked his ground rent theory in the manuscripts for the third volume of the *Capital* (Saito, 2016). Through a theory which has been called the 'metabolic rift' (Foster, 2000; Foster, Clark, & York, 2010), Marx analyzes the depletion of natural resources as the result of the profound inadequacy between the logic of value and the reproduction of non-human life, especially in forestry and farming. With this new perspective in mind, and having taken the results of an emerging ecological science into account,[9] Marx draws a comparison between the capitalist destruction of human and non-human life:

> Moreover, all progress in capitalistic agriculture is a progress in the art, not only of robbing the labourer, but of robbing the soil; all progress in increasing the fertility of the soil for a given time, is a progress towards ruining the lasting sources of that fertility. [...] Capitalist production, therefore, develops technology, and the combining together of various processes into a social whole, only by sapping the original sources of all wealth - the soil and the labourer. (Marx, 1996, pp. 507–508)

In this excerpt, Marx does not only conflate the *exploitation* of work with the *intensive use* of the soil, he also insists on the *exhaustion* of these two sources of wealth, which simultaneously results in their incapacity to reproduce themselves. In capitalist metabolism, life is only valued as the result of abstract labor, just as any other commodity. Insofar as this reduction is blind to the 'autopoiesis' of the living being in its complex connection with an ecosystem, it leads to self-destructive consequences. If this comparison between the exhaustion of human and non-human life under its capitalist form is not only a metaphorical comparison, it remains necessary to analyze the articulation between these two sides of the metabolic process.

In order to overcome the traditional divide between Nature and Society in social sciences, Jason W. Moore proposes the concept of '*oikeios*', thereby interweaving human and non-human life within a same socio-economical form (Moore 2015, pp. 33–49). Applied to a critical study of capitalism, this new theoretical framework is helpful in unfolding the dialectical relation between the destruction of human and non-human life. Early capitalism, based on the accumulation of absolute surplus-value, tended to exhaust human labor-power. Forcing children and women to work intensively, extending the duration of the working day, and compressing wages as much as possible, such an extraction of absolute surplus-value prevented the workers from reproducing themselves.[10] To solve this inner contradiction between the value-form and its basis (human metabolism), capitalism not only restricted its accumulation through a set of labor laws, but also developed a new mode of accumulation of value: relative surplus-value (Marx, 1996, pp. 317–325). Simply put, this concept describes the increase of labor's productivity through new technological input, which enables the production of cheaper commodities necessary for the worker's subsistence; this does not alter the fact that the reproduction of labor-power still depends on a set of reproductive tasks performed by women out of the market, as shown above. However, the counterpart of this growing productivity, allowing higher wages and shorter working days, is an increased appropriation of natural elements (raw materials, energies, land etc.). As Jason Moore puts it, the exploitation of life within waged work is also based on an extended appropriation of life beyond this form:

> Value relations incorporate a double movement of exploitation and appropriation. Within the commodity system, the exploitation of labor-power reigns supreme. But this supremacy is only possible, given its tendency toward self-exhaustion, to the degree that the appropriation of uncommodified natures counteract this tendency. (Moore, 2015, pp. 68–69)

If the accumulation of relative surplus-value, made possible by an increased productivity resolves the first contradiction between the accumulation of absolute surplus-value and the reproduction of labor-power, it also gives birth to a new contradiction between the value-form and the sustainable reproduction of its natural environment.[11]

The latter requires the renewal of raw materials, energies, living beings, and the regeneration of fertile soils necessary to economic production. All these elements represent the result of natural processes independent of human work, but on which capitalism depends to achieve its end. However, the market valuation considers them *only* as the result of abstract labor. In the same ways as for labor-power, the extended natural metabolism is submitted to the law of value, blind to its own dynamic of reproduction. For instance, the exchange-value of timber or oil is only defined by the amount of abstract labor required to extract them, without any consideration for their renewal-rate, or for the atmosphere's capacity to absorb residues of their combustion. The *exhaustion* of natural resources, which originates in this structural abstraction, can partly be overcome by a 'capitalization' of nature, by which natural metabolism really becomes the result of work performed within the 'cash-nexus' (Moore, 2015, p. 111). Not only are hunting and fishing replaced by animal breeding, but the reproduction of life within farming is increasingly the product of human labor enabled by the development of artificial selection and gene technology.

Will this progress in capitalization lead to a true subsumption of nature? In other words, are we to assist in the hegemonic integration of metabolic processes within the value-form? Such a conclusion would turn a blind eye to the limitations and barriers placed on this capitalization of nature to certain domains. For example, the development of the bio-fuels industry, transforming plants into liquid energy, would not be able to replace stocked fossil resources without directly competing with the agricultural production of food. Besides, this integration of natural metabolism within capitalist production remains partial. It fails to take into account the pollution and wastes that result from it – the most disastrous outcome of which is the saturation of the atmosphere by CO_2 causing climate change and global warming (Foster, Clark & York 2010; Malm, 2017). To describe this double process, in which the reproduction of natural conditions of production is undermined both by the exhaustion and the saturation of its metabolism, Jason Moore points out the emergence of a 'negative-value' as the counterpart of the capitalist accumulation of surplus-value (Moore, 2015, pp. 277–278). However, far from being a self-regulating process – the higher costs of natural resources automatically regulating the appropriation of nature – the contradiction between the value-form and the natural conditions of production necessarily entails destructive consequences.[12] Indeed, the temporality of the accumulation process of value and the reproductive process of ecosystems are heterogeneous, so that the negative aftermath of the contradiction arises too late to be taken into consideration by market valuation.

Conclusion

The limitation of the capitalist subsumption of life is twofold: neither the human nor the non-human metabolic processes, on which economic production is based, can be *wholly* integrated in the value-form. However, this unachieved subsumption does not imply the absence of capitalist domination. On the contrary, reproductive work and the free appropriation of nature are both central functions of the capitalist accumulation of surplus-value, precisely *because,* as unpaid externalities, they lower production costs.

Therefore, one should carefully handle the claim that the specific connection of 'women' to 'nature', as mediators of the cycles of the ecosystem's reproduction, represents an economic and political autonomy from capitalist domination. This assumption crystallizes around the emphasis laid on a 'subsistence economy' at the margins of the world-economy, which was defended by the Bielefeld School of ecofeminism (Mies & Bennholdt-Thomsen, 1999) and later developed by Maria Mies in cooperation with Vandana Shiva (2014). They describe the subsistence work performed by women as the remainder of a pre-capitalist mode of production at the margins of the globalized market and a way out of the waged-work system. Such a point of view is however based on the hypothesis that the capitalist form of life is limited to waged-work, and that the separate moment of the metabolic process remains outside of its scope (Scholz, 2011, p. 173). On the contrary, one should underline that the split between two (gendered) forms of life is the very result of the capitalist implementation of the value-form on the reproduction process. Against such a dualistic perspective, we can thus emphasize how both spheres are dialectically intertwined. Hence, within ecofeminist discourse, the definition of women's reproductive activities as natural, or close to nature can be understood as the very result of their partial exclusion from the commodity-market.

Whilst we refuse any essential connection between women and nature, and depart from the idea of a specific connection of women to nature at the margins of the world-economy, we are not condemned to abandoning ecofeminism per se. Even if the emancipation of women from patriarchy and the defense of the environment are not immediately connected, they are negatively related through capitalist domination. As Mary Mellor suggests, there is no essential relation between women and nature, but only a naturalization of certain activities performed by women in a capitalist society.[13] However, due to their social position in the capitalist system, one might emphasize women's privileged standpoint for opposing the destructive domination of nature.

The development of an ecofeminist consciousness is particularly decisive, because of the asymmetrical consequences of the capitalist domination over human and non-human life. Whereas capitalist accumulation is *immediately* dependent on the reproduction of human life, which is the real subject of surplus-value production, it is only *indirectly* dependent on the reproduction of natural environments and non-human life, which are only the objects of surplus-value production. This is why the capitalist economy can tolerate the massive destruction of ecosystems and non-human life forms, insofar as this destruction does not prevent the constant reproduction of human labor-power required for the accumulation of surplus-value. But contrary to women, who can resist their confinement to housework and subjection to patriarchal domination, nature is no political subject per se. It might have an agency as a living totality, but it nevertheless has no political agency, no capacity to resist, to make claims, or to compel a conscious social change (O'Connor, 2011, p. 165). Consequently, the unification of ecological and feminist struggles should be thought of as the development of an oppositional solidarity that doesn't exist prior to but only via political action (Alaimo, 1994, p. 149).

Notes

1. The term 'écoféminisme' was first created by the French author Françoise d'Eaubonne in her book *Le féminisme ou la mort* published in 1970, and was later appropriated by American theorists (Merchant, 2005, p. 193).
2. 'Insofar as the ecofeminist bases for ethics – interconnectedness, aliveness, women's caring – are mediated by the metaphor' women = nature they avoid the problem of the objectivity in the real world. Thus, if an ethics is to be based strictly on metaphors, it becomes wholly tenuous' (Biehl, 1991, p. 24).
3. 'What is at stake in this distinction is the interweaving of the social and the biological within Forms of life, more precisely the integration of Life forms in Forms of life' (Laugier & Ferrarese, 2015, p. 8).
4. In the English edition of the *Capital*, the German word *Stoffwechsel* is vaguely translated by the words 'social interchange'. Such a choice obliterates the chemical background of the original term. It seems more appropriate to translate literally by the word 'metabolism'.
5. Marx himself employed the term of 'reproduction' in both meanings (Marx, 1996, pp. 181, 565). However, while a whole chapter of the *Capital* is dedicated to an analysis of reproduction of social relations of production, his concept of the reproduction of labor-power is largely undertheorized and still framed within an analysis of waged work. As will be shown in the next paragraphs, feminist theory criticizes and overcomes this limitation by a redefinition of reproduction as the result of a specific reproductive work: domestic labor.
6. By analyzing this value-form, Marx differs from the former political economy, which does not distinguish between concrete and abstract labor. Only the latter sets a quantitative equivalent for exchange.
7. According to Marx, the level of necessary human needs never corresponds to a simple biological essence, but always depends on historical and moral determinations (Marx, 1996, p. 181).
8. This theoretical position is illustrated by the work of Christine Delphy. After having insisted on the distinction between the capitalist exploitation of waged work and the patriarchal appropriation of domestic work, she recently departed from the Marxist theory of value on which the critique of exploitation is founded (Delphy, 2015).
9. Although Marx didn't read Haeckel, who used the word 'ecology' for the first time to name the science of the relations of an organism to its environment, he was deeply influenced by his study of the organic chemistry of Justus von Liebig and the physical agriculture of Carl Fraas, who were both pioneers in the scientific analysis of an ecological crisis.
10. On this point, see Marx' historical analysis of the high rate of mortality among the English working class, in the first 19th century: 'What interests [capitalism] is purely and simply the maximum of labour power that can be set in motion in a working-day. It attains this end by shortening the extent of the labourer's life, *as a greedy farmer snatches increased produce from the soil by robbing it of its fertility* [emphasis added]' (Marx, 1996, p. 271).
11. Beside the overproduction crisis, that Marx interprets as the result of an internal economic contradiction, opposing the forces of production and the relations of production, he also considers the possibility of an ecological crisis. It has been theorized as a 'second-contradiction' (O'Connor, 2011) between the economical production and its own conditions: the reproduction of human life as labor power and the reproduction of non-human life as ecosystems.
12. Indeed, the counterpart to the partial integration of life within the capitalist social form is the massive annihilation of non-human forms of life, which has been characterized as the sixth extinction of species: 'Extinction is both the immediate success and ultimate failure of the real subsumption of the earth by the capital' (McBrien, 2016, p. 117).

13. 'Women's identification with the "natural" is not evidence of some timeless unchanging essence, but of the material exploitation of women's work, often without reward.' (Mellor, 1997, p. 189).

Disclosure statement

No potential conflict of interest was reported by the author.

References

Alaimo, S. (1994). Cyborg and ecofeminist interventions: Challenges for an environmental feminism. *Feminist Studies, 20*, 133–152.

Arthur, C. (2004). *The new dialectic and Marx's Capital*. Leiden: Brill.

Backhaus, H.-G. (2011). *Dialektik der Wertform: Untersuchungen zur Marxschen Ökonomiekritik*. Freiburg: Ça ira.

Barrett, M. (2014). *Women's oppression today: The Marxist/feminist encounter*. London: Verso.

Benston, M. (1980). The political economy of women's liberation. In E. Malos (Ed.), *The politics of housework* (pp. 119–129). London: Allison and Busby.

Biehl, J. (1991). *Rethinking ecofeminist politics*. Boston, MA: South End Press.

Bookchin, M. (1971). *Post-scarcity anarchism*. San Fransisco: Remparts Press.

Delphy, C. (2015). *Pour une théorie générale de l'exploitation: Des différentes formes d'extorsion de travail aujourd'hui*. Paris: Syllepse.

Dickenson, D. (2008). *Body shopping: The economy fueled by flesh and blood*. Oxford: Oneworld Publications.

Federici, S. (1975). *Wages against housework*. Bristol: Falling Wall Press.

Foster, J. B. (2000). *Marx's ecology: Materialism and nature*. New York, NY: Monthly Review Press.

Foster, J. B., Clark, B., & York, R. (2010). *The ecological rift: Capitalism's war on the earth*. New York, NY: Monthly Review Press.

Fraser, N. (2014). Behind Marx's hidden abode. For an expanded conception of capitalism. *New Left Review, 86*, 55–73.

Haug, F. (1996). Knabenspiele und Menschheitsarbeit. Geschlechterverhältnisse als Produktionsverhältnisse. In F. Haug (Ed.), *Frauen-Politiken* (pp. 125–151). Hamburg: Argument Verlag.

James, S., & Dalla Costa, M. (1972). *The power of women and the subversion of community*. Bristol: Falling Wall Press.

Laugier, S., & Ferrarese, E. (2015). Politiques des Formes de Vie. [Politics of forms of life] *Raisons Politiques, 57*, 5–12.

Lukács, G. (2011). *Ontologie de l'être social le travail, la reproduction* (N. Tertulian, trans.). Paris: Éditions Delga.

Malm, A. (2017). *Fossil capital: The rise of steam power and the roots of global warming*. London: Verso.

Marx, K. (1973). *Grundrisse: Introduction to the critique of political economy* (M. Nicolaus, trans.). New York, NY: First Vintage.

Marx, K. (1985). *Value, price and profit, Marx & Engels collected works*, Vol. 20. New York, NY: International Publishers.

Marx, K. (1996). *Capital: A critique of political economy vol. I, Marx & Engels Collected works vol. 35*. New York, NY: International Publishers.
Marx, K. (1998). *Capital: A critique of political economy vol. III, Marx & Engels Collected works vol. 37*. New York, NY: International Publishers.
Marx, K., & Engels, F. (1975). *The German ideology*. London: Lawrence & Wishart.
McBrien, J. (2016). Accumulating Extinction: Planetary Catastrophism in the Necrocene. In J. W. Moore (Ed.), *Anthropocene or capitalocene? Nature, history and the crisis of capitalism* (pp. 116–137). Oakland: PM Press.
Mellor, M. (1997). *Feminism and ecology*. Cambridge: Polity Press.
Merchant, C. (2005). *Radical ecology: The search for a livable world*. New York, NY: Taylor & Francis.
Mies, M. (2014). *Patriarchy and accumulation on a world scale: Women in the international division of labour*. London: Zed Books.
Mies, M., & Bennholdt-Thomsen, V. (1999). *The subsistence perspective: Beyond the globalized economy*. Melbourne: Zed Books.
Mies, M., & Shiva, V. (2014). *Ecofeminism*. London: Zed Books.
Moore, J. W. (2015). *Capitalism in the web of life: Ecology and the accumulation of capital*. New York, NY: Verso.
O'Connor, J. (2011). *Natural causes: Essays in ecological Marxism*. New York, NY: Guilford Press.
Saito, K. (2016). *Natur gegen Kapital: Marx' Ökologie in seiner unvollendeten Kritik des Kapitalismus*. Frankfurt: Campus Verlag.
Salleh, A. (1997). *Ecofeminism as politics: Nature, Marx and the postmodern*. New York, NY: Zed Books.
Scholz, R. (2011). *Das Geschlecht des Kapitalismus: Feministische Theorien und die postmoderne Metamorphose des Patriarchats*. Bad Honnef: Horlemann.
Smith, N. (1990). *Uneven development: Nature, capital and the production of space*. Oxford: Blackwell.
Thompson, C. (2005). *Making parents: The ontological choreography of reproductive technologies*. Cambridge: MIT Press.

12 Vocabularies of vulnerability

Sharon P. Holland

> Give me your fingers.
> Under this hair shirt steams the vocabulary
> of flesh, crosshatched into meaning.
> – Vievee Francis, *Horse in the Dark*

This exercise in vocabularies of vulnerability seeks to think through relations among animal, human and black(ness). This exercise is implicitly, though not explicitly related to capital and its flows. As chattel, black (beings) anchor the very machinery of progress in the new world, grounding the creation of a new nation and providing the backbone *against* which conceptualizations of a uniquely American self would be instrumentalized for decades. And in many ways, these anchored understandings of black life and animal life, human and non-human form also prevent us from seeing the extent to which black life has shaped our relationship with animal life. When thinking about the black body *as* animal, we eschew the affective life of relation among human, animal and blackness. We see that capital so shapes the lives of black subjects that we cannot bear a relation outside of those terms. Chattel doesn't world, but then, neither do animals. This is an attempt to rethink this sedimented structure.

There are a myriad or more ways to die in this world and each step over a threshold is a reminder of just how many. From the nightly news to the conference circuit, there is a market – in the flesh, in *discourse* – for vulnerability. Vulnerability is ubiquitous. And it is better still if one can be made vulnerable *to* something or someone. To be (made) vulnerable is to be descended upon by the state, by one's neighbours (remember Derrida's warning about that thing called 'hospitality') or even by the dis-ease of despair. In the wake of Sanford, Florida, Ferguson, Missouri, Staten Island, New York, North Charleston, South Carolina and perhaps little known Bladen County, North Carolina, the work of vulnerability opens up people of color, and for the purposes of my observations here, black people to *a particular* and *constant* scene of racialized violence. Our vulnerability is a narrative told often and always and most importantly it is chosen *for* us. These vocabularies and their attendant narratives tell the story of the indigenous person's archaic-ness, fading into that good night of yesteryear; the Latino/a's foreign-ness, opening an impactful presence to a constant unbelonging; and the black body's collusion with the animal's violence and potentiality for destruction. It is important to note here that I am referring to the stories often told about these communities, rather than to the tales such humans would tell about themselves, or to the ways in which each and every one of the narrative assignments above bleed into one another, as managed life becomes swiftly interchangeable. It does not matter whose body, so long as it is *some*body *other* than you.

To say that blackness/animal/human represents blackness's return to animality would not be accurate without qualification here. What I am driving at is that we need and mean an animality so tied to transgression and excess that the cuteness or cuddliness or the potentiality of the animal to return the human to its humanity is something foreclosed by this necessary ordering. In many ways, the vocabularies used to describe our present state are relentless. I rehearse them here: crisis, catastrophe, terror, nakedness, precarity, perishment, management, sovereignty, and diversity. All vocabularies in capitalism's neoliberal flows. I hope you have noted the inclusion of some of the more benign vocabularies for our global condition. I argue here that these words might do as much to unmake us as do the regimes of power they attempt to illuminate.

Critics have begun the push-back on biopower's catastrophic reach, pulling us all away from the spectacular – known to Lauren Berlant as the 'event' – and back into the quotidian, the ordinary – a space always already thoroughly interrogated by critical race theory since 1973. Having over-indulged in the catastrophic we are now to return to our belief in the efficacy of the everyday. Temporality shifts whenever the possibilities of critical theory are exhausted. More recently, Alexander Weheliye's assessment of black feminism's and by extension, black studies' reach into genres of the human finds biopower, bare life and state of exception lacking. The signal and important contribution here – and I cannot help but think of Charles Mills's work on white supremacy and contract theory in *The Racial Contract* – is that once the theoretical territory is reimagined with the practices of chattel slavery, colonialism and indigenous genocide clearly in our scope, it is therefore possible to imagine a worlding that is other than the order of things so neatly packaged to us as modernity's foothold on the neck of human being. In forgetting these thick-on-the-ground histories of potential conquest, containment and power, critics render the taking of black life unto itself as a natural impossibility. Weheliye's groundbreaking work returns the potentiality of worlding to thresholds of blackness.

In Berlant's assessment of the crisis of crisis (and its management),

> slow death, or the structurally motivated attrition of persons notably because of their membership in certain populations, is neither a state of exception nor the opposite, mere banality, but a domain of revelation where an upsetting scene of living that has been muffled in ordinary consciousness is revealed to be interwoven with ordinary life after all, like ants revealed scurrying under a thoughtlessly lifted rock. (Berlant, 2007, p. 761)

Mobilising 'slow death' as a 'domain of revelation,' Berlant brings us to the ant – a species whose biomass is equal to that of all the humans on the earth, and a species capable of rendering its own members into biopolitical machines (slaves) for the purposes of the colony. I am not sure if Berlant's analogy is intentional, but the muffled living of ants reveals itself as the socio-life, the political life of a species not unlike human being. Moreover, the revelation of political life – bare life – 'revealed ... under a *thoughtlessly* lifted rock' produces human discovery as an oxymoron – a guaranteed but sustained ignorance – a reduced capacity to imagine the possibility of other worlds, other circumlocutions. Moreover, this site now becomes the locus of an '*unsettling* scene of living,' projected onto the colony, revealed to be hidden in plain sight.

In both instances, Berlant and Weheliye move against the notion of precarity, in favour of the episodic in the one instance and the world making capacity of the racial assemblage in the other. These are both brilliant and unsettling accounts of what really comes after the human, if being or becoming human is not our goal. For scholars and critics of biopower and bare life, the threshold is always spectacular, an event (contra Berlant) that moves endangered bodies toward a vulnerability that almost seems like natural selection. The subject never chooses it, that is, it is always random but scripted nonetheless. In short, the kinds of violence that black bodies endure produce a conundrum for basic notions of the human and I will argue at times, temporality itself.

First and foremost, I want to contemplate the possibility of a threshold without such naturalised selection, a threshold where the event upon connection is not only chosen by (black) humanity, but one in which animal being is taken into account, thus opening up the possibility for ethical *and* affective relation. Deleuze and Guattari have defined threshold and self with the following question: 'The self is only a threshold, a door, a becoming between two multiplicities … And at each threshold or door, a new pact?' (Deleuze & Guattari, 1987, p. 275). I take this particular definitional query as instructive because I admire how the self is in fact an opening unto itself; the possibilities of other narratives emerging – even contradictory ones – is kept alive *within* the human capacity to world *even* before one opens the self to the worldview of another. By proliferating the possibilities of contact and (human?) endeavour itself, thus troubling the grounding of progress at the heart of humanity's (constant) overcoming, Deleuze and Guattari produce the work of *being human* as ancillary to work already engaged in and un(der)acknowledged. They open the political's narrow and temporal frame of reference, quite possibility (re)turning our gaze in other (ethical?) directions.

In an earlier iteration of her analysis of species, becoming, thresholds and crossings, Haraway points out the necessity for 'remaining at risk and in solidarity in instrumental relationships that one does not disavow … forgetting the criterion of sharing pain to learn what animals' suffering is and what to do about it is not tolerable anymore, if it ever was' (Haraway, 2008, p. 70). No small irony, at least for my project, that her chapter on laboratory animals opens with an explication of Nancy Farmer's Newbery award-winning novel, *The Girl Named Disaster* whose main character is of African dissent. My point here? That there *are* narratives that place black being, black-ness in direct relation to the animal in modes of consideration, relation and mutual observation that do not always already follow a prescription for violent trespass, possible descent or what I would call negative mimetic relation. When I open up the possibility for ethical relation, therefore, I conversely expose the possibility for spectacular failure as with Derrida and his *c(h)at* in *The Animal That I am Now Following*. I know, in the end that every attempt to arrive at a discourse on the animal, will leave me in the lap of the human every time. But there's no *face* lost in trying, right?

I began this thought-piece with a brief for the animal, a move that might seem out of place if not a bit jarring, because in the vocabularies of vulnerability applied to black agents, we can recognise a constant worry about the descent into animality or simply, being rather than becoming animal. For some, blackness is that shadow of the human waiting to bring itself back from the brink of animality; for others, blackness is the absolute animal that threatens the blood/brain barrier that is the (absolute?) distinction between human and animal. We need to map a relationship among blackness/human/animal that doesn't always already see animality as descent or vulnerability as the negative consequence of biopower – freeing up a bit of space to think about the complexity of human being, the situation of the animal and the conundrum that blackness's affective life presents to a critical world preoccupied with a certain *ordering*.

Like for as

The infamous scene of an almost lynching in the movie adaptation of Solomon Northup's kidnapping into bondage lasts only 2 min and 54 s. I first want to observe that McQueen departs from the established 'slave' narrative that is *Twelve Years a Slave*. I want to ask here too: can it be a 'slave' narrative if the man in question is actually not just free(d), but a free-born subject? But to ask such a question assumes that all of the enslaved are not free. Which begs an answer to yet another question: is all freedom a matter of laws? My point here is that the question of black freedom continues to telescope – one question collapses into another as the condition for human being – to echo Weheliye's brief for black studies – is constantly reset, re-packaged, given the ebb and flow of Circumatlantic tides and global capital.

For Northrup is not twice freed but born free – of free black parents – so his encounter with slavery reverses the first trope of middle passage, placing his captive life here rather than *there*. But I get ahead of myself. The significant departure *here* is that the scene in the published 1853 narrative does not result in such an extended stay at the end of a rope. In Northup's original account, he is tied, the rope is placed around his neck and he is delivered to the base of the tree, but his hanging (but not tying) is forestalled by the appearance of the overseer, Mr. Chapin, who runs off two of the off-plantation thugs who accompany the carpenter and day labourer John Tibeats in his act of revenge for the literal whipping that Northup gives him. In both movie and narrative, Northup escapes his extra-legal death penalty.

The McQueen version is more brutal – it brings our Mr. Northup to the brink of death and at the same time suspends him against and in the forefront of quotidian life – a woman sits preparing dinner in the foreground of one frame. In another instance, children and grownups move from the cabins in the shadow of the columned mansion and go about their play, their tasks. The cruelty of Northup's predicament is heightened by the work and play that takes place around him, as he suffers unto (forestalled) death. In this scene are two kinds of death: one, *extra-legal/state sanctioned* and another, *social* – where the body of the one who has transgressed the law – descended into an animality represented through violent disregard for the rule of law, law of the master, status of the enslaved, as is the case here – is displayed for all to see while at their quotidian lives.

In many ways, McQueen's version of the narrative substantiates the basic underpinnings of what bare life is. *This* Northup can be slaughtered (sacrificed), but he cannot be murdered (have his life taken away from him unjustly). This is precisely the predicament of the enslaved: as property (someone else's life) they can be taken *in sacrifice*, but because they are property under the law, they cannot be murdered by anyone. His potential death must be witnessed by us all, but actually seen by no one – the world we have created must indeed be invisible to all of us. Northrup's struggles at the end of his rope – pun intended – remind us of the desperate flailing of pasterns and hooves in the abattoir, in the slaughterhouse. I am not the first to make this observation of blackness's relationship to the animal in the scene of rendering flesh from bone, disarticulate parts ready for consumption. Charles Burnett gets at this nicely in his brilliant film, *Killer of Sheep* (1978).

A similar sequence opens up the space among human/animal/blackness in Burnett's classic. In juxtaposed scenes of children at play and preparing sheep for slaughter, Burnett deftly comments on the shared space between quotidian life and the possibilities held open by the presence of the slaughterhouse among us. I argue that this space can be read in the service of affective life if we do not mark the animal as worthy of destruction here; if we hold open the possibility for community in the midst of such a catastrophic disaster as the killing floor, then we might be able to think through Burnett's own commentary on the possibilities of human revolutionary space.

Instead of thinking of Northup's treatment as being *like* (that of) an animal – the very meaning of the phrase leaving open the possibility for disregard, the condition that makes the animal always already different from us – something outside the self – we might be inclined to think of Northup's being treated *as* an animal – a semantic ordering that holds open the possibility of ethical relation, of relationship, of, as Donna Haraway reminds us in *Primate Visions, kin*. I am not proposing that we consider 'kin' in the same problematic way in which humanity claimed its great ape cousins – so much of us that they were worth saving. What I am proposing here is that we reconfigure – perhaps that alternate assemblage that critics invoke – the grounding that holds the potentially of connection as an always already troubling decline. What I am looking for here might be that negotiated space – something the late Jose Munoz once called, after Gramsci, hegemony. A relationship not set in line with the (perfect) order of things, but one in which two beings in close proximity (a precarious concept as well, by the way) create the possibility of (an)other world(s). A way to be vulnerable outside the limited possibilities that capitalism presents to us.

Disclosure statement

No potential conflict of interest was reported by the author.

References

Berlant, L. (2007). Slow death (sovereignty, obesity, lateral agency). *Critical Inquiry, 33*, 754–780.

Deleuze, G., & Guattari, F. (1987). *A thousand plateaus: Capitalism and schizophrenia*. (B. Massumi, Trans.). Minneapolis: University of Minnesota Press.

Haraway, D. (2008). *When species meet*. Minneapolis, MN: University of Minnesota Press.

Index

www.ingramcontent.com/pod-product-compliance
Lightning Source LLC
LaVergne TN
LVHW080658011026
849160LV00014B/1472